CUMBRIA HERITAGE SERVICES
LIBRARIES

This book is due to be returned on or before the last date above. It may be renewed by personal application, post or telephone, if not in demand.

C.L.18

Barry MacSweeney: Bibliography

POETRY

The Boy from the Green Cabaret Tells of His Mother
(Hutchinson, 1968; McKay, New York, 1969)
The Last Bud (Blacksuede Boot Press, 1969)
Joint Effort, with Pete Bland (Blacksuede Boot Press, 1970)
Flames on the Beach at Viareggio (Blacksuede Boot Press, 1970)
Our Mutual Scarlet Boulevard (Fulcrum Press, 1971)
12 Poems and a Letter, with Elaine Randell (Curiously Strong, 1971)
*Just 22 and I Don't Mind Dyin': The Official Poetical Biography
    of Jim Morrison, Rock Idol* (Curiously Strong, 1971; Turpin Press, 1973)
Brother Wolf (Turret Press, 1972)
Fools Gold (Blacksuede Boot Press, 1972)
Five Odes (Transgravity Advertiser, 1972)
Dance Steps (Joe Dimaggio Publications, 1972)
Six Odes (Ted Kavanagh Books, 1973)
Fog Eye (Ted Kavanagh Books, 1973)
Black Torch (New London Pride Editions, 1977)
Far Cliff Babylon (Writers' Forum, 1978)
Odes (Trigram Press, 1978)
Blackbird [Book 2 of *Black Torch*] (Pig Press, 1980)
Starry Messenger (Secret Books, 1980)
Colonel B (Colin Simms, 1980)
Ranter (Slow Dancer Press, 1985)
The Tempers of Hazard, with Thomas A. Clark & Chris Torrance
    (Paladin Re/Active Anthology No.3, published & destroyed 1993)
Hellhound Memos (Many Press, 1993)
Pearl (Equipage, 1995)
Zero Hero in *etruscan reader III* (etruscan books, 1996; republished 1997)
    [with 'Finnbar's Lament' and 'Blackbird' from *The Tempers of Hazard*]
The Book of Demons [with *Pearl*] (Bloodaxe Books, 1997)

PROSE

Elegy for January: A Life of Thomas Chatterton, Newcastle University
    Literature Lecture (Menard Press, 1970)

POETRY/ARTWORK

Your Father's Plastic Poppy, 12 silkscreen prints with artist Roger Lunn
    (Goldsmiths' College, London, 1969)
Ode to Coal, poetry poster (South East Arts, 1978)

THE BOOK OF DEMONS

DEMONS

Barry MacSweeney

BLOODAXE BOOKS

ISBN: 1 85224 414 3

First published 1997 by
Bloodaxe Books Ltd,
P.O. Box 1SN,
Newcastle upon Tyne NE99 1SN.

Bloodaxe Books Ltd acknowledges
the financial assistance of Northern Arts.

Cover printing by J. Thomson Colour Printers Ltd, Glasgow.

Printed in Great Britain by
Cromwell Press Ltd, Broughton Gifford, Melksham, Wiltshire.

for Jackie Litherland
beloved comrade and warrior queen

Acknowledgements

Pearl was first published in full by Equipage (Cambridge) in 1995. These poems first appeared in anthologies published by the 6 Towns Poetry Festival (1993-96): 'No Buses To Damascus' in *Peacocks Two*; 'Pearl Against The Barbed Wire' in *Peacock Blue*; 'Blizzard: So Much Bad Fortune', 'Cavalry At Calvary', 'Fever', 'Pearl Suddenly Awake', 'Sweet Jesus: Pearl's Prayer', 'Looking Down From The West Window', 'Shreds Of Mercy/The Merest Shame' and 'Daddy Wants To Murder Me' in *Ink Feathers*; and 'Demons Swarm Upon Our Man And Tell The World He's Lost' in *Etruscan Jetty*. The sequence *Zero Hero* (which includes the poems 'Strap Down In Snowville', 'Sweeno, Sweeno', 'Up A Height And Raining' and 'Tom In The Market Square Outside Boots') was a 6 Towns Poetry Festival commission for *For the Locker and the Steerer*, published in *etruscan reader III*, with Maggie O'Sullivan and David Gascoyne (etruscan books, 1996; republished 1997). Several poems from *Pearl* and *The Book of Demons* were first published in *Object Permanence* and *Angel Exhaust*. 'Ode To Beauty Strength And Joy And In Memory Of The Demons' first appeared in *Iron*.

The author would like to thank Northern Arts for a Writer's Award granted for *Pearl* in 1995; the following year the book won a prize in the Northern Electric Arts Awards. Special thanks are also due to The Royal Literary Fund and The Society of Authors for substantial financial support which enabled him to attend Farm Place addiction clinic for two months, and to receive aftercare treatment.

Contents

PEARL

Looking Down From The West Window

I smashed my wings
against the rain-soaked deck
and was happy you lifted me
into your safe fingers and palms.
If not too disgusted, hold me
close forever keenly.

Sweet Jesus: Pearl's Prayer

Listen, hark, attend; wait a moment
as they used to say
in the ancient tongue of literacy, before
language was poisoned to a wreckage, which
you will find for a fee (going up)
in your earpiece, inside
the wainscoted foyer
of the Museum of Stupidity down in the dumps:
Permit me to say this on a grey roofslate, as I protect
my poor writing, I can't do joined up, with soaked forearm
from the driving rain – I am Pearl.
Please estrange your children, and your bairns' bairns
from terrible tabloidations, scored into
your blood in the sorriest ink.
O paranoid Marxist Cambridge prefects,
self-appointed guarantors of consonants and vowels
and arrangement of everyday sentences, placing
of punctuation marks, with which Pearl
wished to be in steady flux, she said
with fingers, eyes, thumbs and palms. Listen.

When the borage flowers closed at night
she moved against me, rain lashed facing
west to the law, whispering: There is so much
wickedness.
They want to tax my ABC, they want to jail my tongue.
I dream their high-up heather deaths
though I do not emit articulate sound.
I am just a common white swan.
Fierce I am when I want, want
my milky hands on my destroyers, rive
them apart like a marauding riever, or
down south, roll you in the Nene, without
Dunlop lace-up boots, one bare foot
should do it, spate or trickle you'll be face down.
Spade job later, midnight special, I've got
one somewhere, I know mam has; bury
you all deep, lead tunnels or out on the Fens.

I cannot cease to dream and speak of Pearl.

Pearl's Utter Brilliance

Argent moon with bruised shawl
discreetly shines upon my frozen tongue tonight
and I am grinning handclap glad.
We loved so much the lunar light
on rawbone law or splashing in the marigold beds,
our gazing faces broken in the stream.
Taut, not taught, being kept from school
was a disgrace, single word 'idiot' chalked
on the yard wall: soaked in sleet, sliding
in snow beneath a raft of sighs, waiting
for the roar of an engine revved before
daybreak, as the world, the permanent wound
I would never know in sentence construction, fled
away from my heather-crashing feet, splash happy
kneefalls along the tumblestones,
whip-winged plovers shattering the dew.
Each day up here I am fiercely addressed
by the tips of the trees; said all I could
while heifers moaned in the stalls, clopping
of hooves my steaming, shitting
beast accompaniment. And these giant clouds.
Pity? Put it in the slurry with the rest of your woes.
I am Pearl, queen of the dale.

Pearl Says

Down from the rain-soaked law
and the rim of the world
where even on misty nights
I can see the little lights
of Penrith and Kendal and, yes,
Appleby, and hear the clatter of unshoed
horses which pound like my heart,
I also sense the moss greened underwater
stones of the Eden to the west. I trim
the wick for mam's asleep now, dad
long gone to Cumberland and work, and
read read my exercise books filled
with stories by Bar, my trout-catching
hero, dragons and space ships, sketches
in crayons you can't buy anymore.
When I stand on the top road and bow
in sleet, knuckle-bunching cold, or
slide over dead nettles on snow, do
not mistake my flung out silhouetted
limbs for distant arches and viaducts.
I am not bringing you legendary feats
of sophisticated engineering. I in
worry eat my fist, soak my sandwich
in saliva, chew my lip a thousand times
without any bought impediment. Please
believe me when my mind says and
my eyes send telegraphs: I am Pearl.
So low a nobody I am beneath the cowslip's
shadow, next to the heifers' hooves.
I have a roof over my head, but none
in my mouth. All my words are homeless.

No Such Thing

Grassblade glintstreak in one of the last mornings
before I come to meet you, Pearl,
as the rain shies. How bright and sudden the dogrose,
briefly touched by dew, flaming
between the deep emerald and smoky blue.
Dogrose, pink as Pearl's lips, no
lipstick required, what's that mam, no
city chemist or salon. We set
our colour charts in the rain
by feldspar heaved from the streambed;
cusloppe, burn peat in summer
and wild trampled marigolds.
Pearl, somewhere there is a stern receiver
and all accounts are open in the rain.
Once more through the heifer muck
and into the brilliant cooling of the watermint beds.
Sky to the west today, where you are, Pearl, is
a fantastic freak bruise which hurts the world.
Coward rain scared of our joy refuses to come.
Deep despair destroys and dents delight
now that I have pledged my future to you, Pearl,
from the edge of the roaring bypass, from
the home of the broken bottle and fiery
battleground of the sieged estate.

Mony Ryal Ray

For urthely herte myght not suffyse
– PERLE

Skybrightness drove me
to the cool of the lake
to muscle the wind
and wrestle the clouds
and forever dream of Pearl.
O Pearl, to speak in sentences, using
all the best vowels and consonants, is argent sure.
Smoke drifts over slow as Pearl's fingers
fanning through the borage groves
and the world vigorous again
in pursuit of renewal.
Pearl into Hexham
with cleft palate: the market, into Robbs
for curtains believe it or not, orders
written out by mam to be handed over, post
office adjacent to the war memorial,
bus station.
Billy driving Pearl home on the Allenheads bus, off
here, pet?, and round
the turning circle
by the heritage centre
to be opened by an adulterous prince.
Pearl saying when asked by a dale stranger,
'Where's the way to The Grapes?':
a-a-a-a-a-a-a-.

Only the magnificent peewit more eloquent than Pearl.

No Buses To Damascus

Wonder Pearl distemper pale, queen
of Blanchland who rode mare Bonny
by stooks and stiles in the land
of waving wings and borage blue
and striving storms of stalks and stems.
Pearl, who could not speak, eventually
wrote: Your family feuds are ludicrous.
Only my eyes can laugh at you.
She handed over springwater under a stern look.
We fell asleep at Blackbird Ford
named by princes Bar and Paul of Sparty Lea.
We splashed and swam and made the brown trout mad.
Dawdled in our never-ending pleasure over
earth-enfolded sheephorns
by rivermist webs, half-hidden moss crowns.

Up a height or down the dale in mist or shine
in heather or heifer-trampled marigold
the curlew-broken silence sang its volumes.
Leaning on the lichen on the Leadgate Road,
Pearl said: a-a-a-a-a-, pointing with perfectly poised
index finger towards the rusty coloured dry stone wall
which contrasted so strongly with her milky skin.

The congenital fissure in the roof of her mouth
laid down with priceless gems, beaten lustrous copper
and barely hidden seams of gold.

Pearl Suddenly Awake

Banged my right hand
against the chipped middle drawer
in the corner of the west-facing bedroom, sucking
home the knuckle blood.
Once more I rose
and kneeled, praying to God, and rose again,
my tongue in everlasting chains.
Bless him asleep with his yellow hair,
worn out with wandering, map-reading
the laws and lanes and trails.
Cowslips, our rushing ancient stream,
years of rain sweeping over the cairns,
beautifully soft, distinctly-shaped moss and lichen
enfolding the retrieved tumblestones,
steps to our great and mad adventures.
We laughed off cuts and bruises falling in the tadpole pools.
In my mind at the top of the valley,
roar of lead ore poured crashing
into the ghosts of now forsaken four-wheeled bogies
distinctly off the rails. They –
you call it government – are killing everything
now. Hard hats abandoned in heather. Locked-up
company huts
useless to bird, beast or humankind. Tags
in the rims: Ridley, Marshall,
McKinnon and Smith. Deserted
disconnected telephones, codes
and names I could not read.
Dead wires
left harping in the high wind
that always sang to me.
Day dawn dripping of dew
from those greenly dark feathers of fern, beneath
fragrant needles of fir and pine
as the stars swing into place
above our double gaze at heaven.

Fever

Pearl, I'm singing Fever to you
but still in the bland auditorium the stupid voices explode.
No one but you is listening.
We are back in the sheepfield chasing a rabbit again.
The rain is from the dark west tonight, raced along
by the sharply pushed-out breath of Pearl.
She has tramped with her cleft to the law, soaked cairn,
OS number recorded once for future use
but forgotten in the slap of heifer rumps.
In her little-fingered grip of the full-buttoned coat,
hair maddened by such a storm, lips pursed; my heroine, not
bothered with Kendal Mintcake, tugger of shirts and cuffs and hair.
She opens her swan mouth and rain pours in from north
and south and west, Atlantic squalls from Donegal.
They cannot lubricate her speech.
A baked canyon there, my Pearl.
At 3 I woke, rolled and twisted all my milky wrists
around the iron bedposts, heart ransomed to Pearl, her
Woolworth butterfly blue plastic clip, still made in Britain
then, her flighty bow.
Due east she looks, lashed by rain one side, yonder
just mist wet, heather splashes in the gale, towards the broken
ovens of manufacture and employment, and to the new units
in green and red, with almost literate noticeboards,
development corporation
fast-growing shrubs (emerald tops and silver undersides:
pound notes with roots), not with
the tramp, tramp, tramp
of men and women going home.
Transport of the rain where Pearl is, is
taken care of forever,
long after we have gone, into the cracked peat
we have not cut, taken to the channels,
onto becks and springs, to the borage groves
and streaming watermint.
At 4 I woke again
with torment, unpunished badness and unjudged blame.
That night, Pearl faced the lightning alone.
She could not even speak to encourage her own bravery.
Last seen by me tongue far out as it would go
just acting like a gutter or a gargoyle
praying for St Elmo's fire up here on the Cushat Law
to surge her diction down the alphabet trail.

The Shells Her Auburn Hair Did Show

(for Stephen Bierley)

Good morning Pearl, good morning John,
good morning the Jesus Christ Almighty;
good morning Stephen, transferring
to the Alps from Lac de Madine:
I know your heart's in Helpston today.
Pearl walked barefoot down the rain-soaked flags last night, fearful
of smoke and fire, with words on the slate: Where do I go
to bang MY head? Where will I find a workshop
sustained by Strasbourg grants
and European funny money, with instruments
modern enough to replace the canyon in the roof of my mouth?
Government? What does that mean?
Stephen, best friend of Barry, travelling in France, father
of Rachel and Timothy, husband of Sarah, what
does a government do? Can it make you speak?
I leak truth like a wound, sore not seen to.
Call me a scab if you wish, I'm still plain Pearl.
Wild Knitting was named after me, I know you did, Bar.
Every day – I wake at four – tongue fever grasps me
and I am possessed: though
my screen is blank and charmless to the human core
I have an unbending desire to marry consonants and vowels
and mate them together
in what you call phrases and sentences
which can become – imagine it – books!
I'd like to sit down with Stephen, inside the borage groves, sing him
my songs of the stream.
But of course I cannot.
My cuticles above singular fields
of harvested grain, when torched stubble is nowhere
near the heat of the burning grief
in my illiterate heart, when I can only hope to extinguish it
with unfettered tears, at four in the morning, when no one else
is awake.
I walk to the wetted garden where the lawn is short.
All the skies are leased anyway. Nothing is owned
by humans. It is an illusion nightmare.
You fall through the universe
clinging to unravelled knots and breaking strings.
John eating grass. Percy drinking brine.
No B&Q in my day. No proper ABC.

My mouth a wind-tunnel. I flew like a moth in its blast.
Take my hand and put me right.
This is the end of the bulletin from the end of the road.

Pearl Alone

Yes, I am not emitting articulate sound.
I take my stand and – deliberately – refuse to plead.
There is no adoration in my mute appeal.
My tongue a pad or cone for the trumpet's bell.
Tongue-tied, bereft of ABC, I lap
and soak my whistle at the law's rim.
In mood moments
I say smash down the chalkboard:
let it stay black.
Shake my chained tongue, I'll fake a growl – a-a-a-a-a-.
Dog my steps, I am wet-toed to the spring
for mam's tea: spam on Sundays
and chips if there is coal.
In the Orient I would be a good servant
willing to please.
Damping of strings my speciality,
an hired mourner
for the rest of my days: gazer
at umbrellas and rain.
No use for owt else up here
except wiping my legs of heifer muck
and fetching the four o'clock milk.
In the byre alone I weep
at the imagined contrivance
of straps and wires
locking my loll-tongue gargoyle head.
My muzzle gushes rain
and I wince when people speak to mam,
giving me their sideways look.
My eyes go furious and I stamp, stamp, stamp.
Pulse fever even in Hartfell sleet.
Loud tumult, what there is of my mind
tumbled into the lashing trees. Yes,
I love falling, caught momentarily
through each tall command of branches, amazed once more
at the borage blue sky
in another September afternoon
with tongue spouting, soaking the cones, thudding
to the very ground, disturbing
all the birds and worms and wasps and bees.
Don't count on me for fun
among the towering cowslips,
but please don't crush my heart.

Cavalry At Calvary

(for Maggie O'Kane)

All aboard, it's party time, with
my averring slut receptionist.
In the land of panty punishment,
she's king.
I traipsed around in belting sleet
the glades and glens
searching my ghost of Pearl.
Pearl in borage by the tadpole pool.
Pearl on the law, hair lashed backward,
facing the great west wind
from Alston and Nenthead.
Pearl on Noble's trailer, squinting into the sun,
lambing done for the day.
Then I lost my mind in Sarajevo: twice, every night.
I was all hitched up with a dying beauty, Irma Hadzimuratovic,
across four columns, 12 cems deep, final edition. She was stable
at the time
but I could not stop dreaming of Pearl,
her bare feet driving the brown trout mad.
We were Herculesed out of Sarajevo, terrifically
muscular, Spielberg almost, and
everyone spoke of us in harried whispers,
7, 9, or 10 o'clock tones, we were moved around
like pit pony adverts, double column change please, page nine.
Panic over, the doctor said.
Irma, I know the surgeons have rebuilt your bowels and your back.
Irma, in the agony of the night, in the filthy bombshell bombhell,
under the nostrils of the TV cameras, freak show
brilliance, foaming at the mouth
for the worldwide page of the *Shields Gazette*, baby. Irma,
dying on your little side, arm the colour of fresh milk.
Irma, page one if there's nowt better, pet,
for this edition only,
I love you today as much as Pearl.

From The Land Of Tumblestones

O the rare gold
under the tips of the trees.
October the long shadows, new jobs with the power station
over the law, strange restlessness of winter, ovens
long closed down the dale.
The cold-blooded couriers of planned unemployment
were not then in full station.
Again I woke at four, sky tar-black, then the bull
over Africa, and heard him go, quarter-ironed,
thunder-heeled to the west, to Penrith and Appleby, Olympia
hammering out chrysanthemum and leek show results.
Long time over the law he was back, longing
for my saliva-gushing tongue, my path spittle,
my bright-eyed, brown-eyed face, my grip fingers
when berry collecting, red or blue, in our
upland empire.
I moved my hands in little mitts as best I could.
We strode together daily
over sullen ghosts of lead,
the boom of collapsed shafts,
no longer mastered by men. Cold ovens.
Borage groves sawn down by Jack
in the night.
Eventually I would write, not say,
I loved you, special consonants and vowels
recorded on paper up here
in the high country: white water,
foaming tumblestones, wet and grey days, or
brilliant Aprils and Septembers, shine, shine, shine,
I loved you absolutely all of the time.

Dark Was The Night And Cold Was The Ground

Pearl: beautiful lustre, highly prized gem,
precious one, finest example of its kind,
dewdrop, tear of Mary, reduced by attrition
to small-rounded grains.
Pearl in the Borage up to her waist.
Pearl in the wildmint.
Pearl in the wind-spilled water.
Pearl flecked in the sunlight, one
foot here, one there, knuckles on hips
on the stile, all angles and charms.
Pearl adrift in the rain through the whispering burn.
So much sighing at her own distress: a-a-a-a-a-.
Pearl looks in the mirror of the molten water,
sticks out her tongue and all you get
is a splash on the path.
I looked into her face and was humbled once again.
Lipstick, she said, on a slate in the rain,
is a complete nobody to me.
I'd like a square meal daily
for me and my mam.

Pearl And Barry Pick Rosehips For The Good Of The Country

Hammers and pinions, sockets, fatal faces
and broken bones. That was after Pearl.
All mornings the sapphire sky, judge wig clouds, here
to Dunbar, made especially gentle because
turned left towards Ireland and soft rain, air delicious
with scent of borage and thyme, dreaming, dreaming,
dreaming and dreaming of Pearl. She gripped her Co-op coat
and she gripped me, bonds not lost in azure eternity.
When yearning for correct connections
of consonants and vowels, verbal vagaries not excluded,
taking into addition
my often gobsmacked face, when I did not tug
fast enough pointing to the dipper's nest.
We went to pick rosehips in the upland raw, above
the whitewater and the falling tumblestones.
Blue days raced by like a Hexham builder's van
late for lunch. We crushed a heady brew
of grass and fern, and loved the slate grey rain.

Surge, surge, I feel today, in the law drizzle, after
tugging my Bar, but my tongue won't move.
I am just a strange beak, purring with my fruit.
Open my mouth and water fountains down.
I am responsible for the pool on the path.

She had the most amazing eyes in history.

Those Sandmartin Tails

(for Holly Hunter)

I could never speak.
What good was I to anyone?
I have, I learned later, the emotions
of literate people: joyed when it shined, sun
so fierce in the molten white water it took my breath away.
I washed my hair beneath the ice-cold tumblestones.
At night the wide-awake dream – waterproof
lace-up Dunlop boots.
We stretched our limbs in sheets of rain
on the Killhope or Cushat, thumbing and fingering
rain off our west-facing faces.
Donegal sleet spoke to our faces uniquely,
eyes a furnace of hazel and blue.
Pearl I was and am, standing alone
in the October spokeshadows of the hospital trees.
Pearl I was and am, firm fingered with nails
well cut, red mittens and bright smiles, alone
in the streambed, feldspar and quartz, no words available.
Deftly-ladled ankles, thanks to God, opal
in the law light, toes wetted in the berylmintbed.
Frost on the earth stiffens my clicking backdoor tongue,
and despite the joy of a surging stream
it is late and my soul is dark.

Woe, Woe, Woe
(for Jim Greenhalf)

All of you with consonants and vowels
and particular arrangement of phrases and sentences
spoken and written, should have seen my eyebrows
move around, my hands and arms go crazy.
Not least you saw me lick the drizzle
from the aching door post I leaned against,
thinking it would lubricate my poorly-engineered tongue.
Many of you shied away
but it was really me who had the hurt
as the argent rising moon looked in.
I had a little Woolworth blackboard
and the heathens want to tax my ABC.
I move my outstretched fingers gently, natural
in a long-grassed, wind-moved world
under this cobalt sky: O what delight
to hear the dippers up the road
drinking in an April morning.
Yes, yes, it is true: I am always worried,
fretting by the gate at the turn in the lane.
All of that law rain soaking my face
upturned to heaven. Once more a prayer unsaid.
I can be fierce nonetheless
to help hug against the many sores.
Hands, palms, right and left, hardened
by bucket-filling, bucket-fetching,
bringing spring water for mam, slopping out beast clarts.
Sick of it sometimes in the hard dark mornings
and unable to adequately say so
I throw the pails helter-skelter into the stinking drain hole,
smiling quietly for you only.

Blizzard: So Much Bad Fortune

(for Jackie Litherland)

I tear apart the smart brochures
in my fit, my ABC war.
Wind heaving tonight in the red berries and branches.
Lit windows suddenly revealed in their stone shoulders.
Halt I am with alphabet arrest, up
a height in the snow my croaking throat soaked.
Argent water hurled against the shifting tumblestones.
Fierce bidding for space between me and the gale.
Idiot, the wall said. Person so deficient in mind
as to be permanently incapable of rational conduct;
colloquial: stupid person.
My tongue abandoned with unmade key.
In my brain a terrible country, violent and wild.
All those unspaced paving stones,
all those untravelled distances,
all of those sentences frozen in time.
I can say less than a dog.
Hailstones from Ireland and America thrown in my face,
a duly convicted human full stop.
In fragrant marigold heaven
then I am not so fierce, so tongue-blind, dreaming
of telling dales tales to who will listen,
hands in the borage, toes in the watermint.
The curlew's cry my daily ode to beauty and delight.
Is not the peewit's high-up heather song all poetry to me?

Lost Pearl

My hands are in the clouds again, thumping the sun.
And then I would be a wild, not mild, child,
stamping my feet and cry, cry, cry,
looking up at the mesmeric flicker of adult mouths
as they said A and E and I and U and O, all joined up
in terrible tresses, looking down at me,
not quite forgiving mam my swollen grave inconsequence.
I held myself in a corner laughing
when they moved around their pretty vowels and consonants.
Outside, are they blisters of hurt on the moon?
Or the rims of craters before you fall defeated
with the dogs on your blood?
Will I return forty years from now – 1998 –
to find the chalkboard frozen, nibs
broken, inkwell shards scattered to four walls
by Irish gales, through shattered windows, and
no one ready to pick up a pen to say this:
sentences are not for prisoners only.
Now I will circle and uncircle
my index fingers forever alone
in the pools, spelling and unspelling
our tragic consequences, smiling
then not smiling, sunshine on
borage and the restless waves of bees,
rain and the silenced creak of the
stile gate, because of the mixture
of oil, dripped in the hinges
from the emerald painted neck
of the spoon-armed, thin nozzled
drip-drop oil can – Castrol – and, yes, my dear,
thank you for helping me over.
We walked there and nearby always so very kindly.

Pearl's Poem Of Joy And Treasure

Spout, pout, spout. Put my spittle all about.
Bare feet pressing down wet upon the glamorous
deciduous rugs of gold. Otherwise
needles and cones, sheep bones, crisps
and ox-cheek for tea.
Dark despair around benights me.
Above the burn I listen for the turn
of the water over tumblestones,
wag my tongue like a wand
in the law wind. Fierce light
invades my eyes and shut face, closed for the night.
Unable to sleep, despite the hardness of the day,
I cluck and purr.
Why am I ashamed of my permanent silence?
In the brilliant heather, shin deep, I am
a good lass, purring and foaming, friend of green breasted
plover, keen listener to the wind in the wires; all
the bees and beasts understand
my milky fingers and palms.
I whet my whistle in the same pools –
at one with the world.
This white water upland empire, hidden
moss grows in the cracks.
I felt my way there when climbing
the bank, press my head there, soft emerald cushions,
when summer sleep takes on.
The wind runs and roars from the west, from the ferry landings
of Ireland; I listen for the freshly falling tumblestones,
long and long until tears almost drown me
for consonants and vowels, sentences of good measure,
for an understanding of the very word syntax, brought
to my cavernous mouth, practising the words Appleby, Penrith, Shap.
Rosehip plucker, mitts needing repair,
here mam, on the sideboard, longing
for the words capital letter, Ordnance Survey map, to
read the true height of the law, emphasise my longing.
Twine my tongue and ease its itch.
Make the sky so borage blue.
Let the argent stars shine upon my upturned smiling face
and furnish me with hope.
I need all the love I can hold.

Pearl At 4am

Moon afloat, drunken opal shuggy boat
in an ocean of planets and stars.
Fierce clouds gather over me
like a plaid shawl.
Gone, gone, click of quarter irons
to Nenthead, Alston and beyond.
I moved my mouth in the darkness of the kitchen,
spittle poured wrongfully into the pan fat.
Snow once more
in my broken face, reduced
to licking the swollen door post. Just a gargoyle.
Death upon us like a stalking foot-soldier, high
and mighty on the law, bayonet
fixed. A sudden glint there, and that's it.
Spluttering lard
and strange sparks
ignite my mind, for I am in love
with something I do not know.
It is the brusque wind,
the nearest falling tumblestones
dislodged by the spate, the finest
snowdrops under heaven.

Pearl's Final Say-So

Fusillade of the sun's eye-piercing darts.
Then sky from Dunbar and the long curve strands
arrives laden with rain: O these winds which move
my golden hair and heart and the fierce tips
of my beloved whispering trees.
The damage has been done with moon-kissed me, running
and racing downhill, flung beside myself
with silence or groans into clart-filled ditches and drains.
Where is my fierce-eyed word warrior today? Slap with violence
all you wish night and day, my language Lancelot − left hand
margin Olympia 5022813 − ABC impossible − and
I struggle and struggle but mean to win my way in
(cat, sat, bat, mat!): only the peewit,
the puffed lark − look at him rise ardent-breasted
as the tractor comes by − and chough with poetry
in the grass-turning, wind-burning morning. Say Nowt.
Sun and rain, wild perfume in my poor clothes
from heather and bilberry and the faint remaining
smell of sheep-dip on my neatly-sewn hem by mam, all wild
as anything on the Cushat. Then as the great winds sweep
across my frozen tongue I lean and lie and weep
for want of proper placing of full stops and all other means
of regular punctuation; I draw them in the grass
but the wind just drives them away from me. Wet-footed
I tread home alone as the beasts are put in and the byres closed.
Lance, lance, Lancelot, let me practise that, index fingers
working the keys, corporal acting as sergeant: yes, leave
your argent blade inside my aching brain, its light
will help me find the way towards the proper letters of my ABC −
for I am Pearl, idiot by ford and stile, stile which does
not squeak now, idiot awash beneath the tumblestones,
receiver and glad conjuror of hailstones from the law
whose inevitable forwarding address is my face and knuckles
and who will forever be the agents which cool my blood.
And mam has let the stove die − not like her − so it is cold tonight.
Typewriter he taught me down the dale − mitts on − Red mittens −
and the sun's last lances lingering lovingly in Penrith
& Kirkby Stephen, where clatter of brief-legged ponies
hammered in my heart, but mossbank stones pillowed my spirit:
before the awesome black velvet went over my eyes
up a height in the last wilderness on the frozen law.
Those faraway jewels and halo brooches rived from darkness:
Stars!

THE BOOK OF DEMONS

Ode To Beauty Strength And Joy And In Memory Of The Demons
(for Jackie Litherland)

1

Forgive me for my almost unforgiveable delay – I have been laying the world
                                                to waste
        beyond any faintest signal of former recognition. For a start, a very
                                        brief beginning
on my relentless destruction trail, I made the dole queues longer for they did not
        circle the earth in the dire band of misery I had wished and hoped
                                                before my
        rise to power among the global demons.
    All my demons, my demonic hordes, reborn Stasi KGB neck-twisters
and finger crushers, their overcoats the width of castles
        fashioned from the skins of Jews and poets, rustle with a fearful symphony
                within the plate-sized buttons, rustling pipistrelles
                        and other lampshade bats. Some carry zipper body bags,
                black and gleaming in the acid rain, from the mouths of others
                words in Cyrillic Venusian torture chamber argot
                stream upwards red on banners backwards
                in a pullet neck-breaking snap in the final perversion
                        of the greatest revolutionary poster that
                        ever lived: the Suprematist Heart.
            And don't forget, he will not let you forget, the man with the final
                beckon, the forefinger locked in deadly
                        fearful invite. This demon, this gem-hard
            hearted agent of my worst nightmare, this MC with spuriously
            disguised gesture, this orchestrator of ultimate hatred,
                        the man with no eyes, no cranium, no brow no hair.
    He will always be known as the Demon with the Mouth of Rustling
            Knives, and the meshing and unmeshing blades
                        are right in your face. The blades say: there are your
                    bags. Pack them and come with us. Bring your bottles
                    and leave her. The contract is: you drink, we don't. The
            rustling bats stay sober. When drunk enough they gather on your face
            and you stand upon the parapet. You sway here and she is utterly
                                                forgotten.
        All that matters are the sober bats and the lampshade overcoats, which
press towards the edge above the swollen tide. You jump, weighed with
    empty bottles in a number of bags – some hidden as it happens of which
    you were ashamed inside your stupid sobering torment. And of course
    we jump, arms all linked, with you into the fatal tidal reach. We also
        pay a price. But the demon who shall always be known as the Mouth
of Rustling and Restless Knives, he stands upon the parapet. Never dies.
    And all that can be heard beyond the wind are the relentless blades.

2

And then there is the pure transmission of kissing you, when
solar winds seethe in amber wonder through the most invisible wisps
    and strands in a tender half-lit prairie sometimes, caught in
light which is not quite light, but as if the entire world was drenched slate,
    or reflected thereof, in the soon to be handsome dawn of a reckless
damp November, with the gunmetal heavens plated quite beautifully
    in goldleaf of fallen nature already so readily ready for the rising
sap of a dearest darling spring when we will start again and the curtains
    will not be drawn at dawn beneath the monumental viaduct of the
great engineer. The truly great span of the legs above the city, spread
    and wide, rodded north and south and electrified by power passing
through beneath the novas and planets and starres. Magnetised!

Free Pet With Every Cage

Get out the shotgun put it in the gunrack.
Here I am gargoyled and gargled out,
foam then blood,
Flatface to Nilsville. In the toe-tag toerag dark,
siege upon his paling, wires berserk like cyborg fingers
in the demon neon's placid acid rain.
All the faery cars are shattered, overparked.
This is the hell time of the final testament,
the ultimate booking, the whipped out ticket, little Hitler
with Spitfire pencil on permanent jack-up; when he's not red
carding
your fanned-out fucked-up Bournville chocolate cheekbones
he's planning an invasion down your throat.
Big Jack with the bad crack,
just so peak and gleaming visor, ferret eyes
glinty like fresh poured Tizer – the seepage of the coleslaw,
the duff mayonnaise.
This is the season of firestorm lightning, torment time
of hell is beautiful.
Wide-awake hell, hell with fingers in a tightened vice,
forget the armies of little white mice,
hell beribboned with garotted larks and lice.
Yes, hell is beautiful, the weirdest ABC ever spoken
here in the dead letter box
in Crap Future Lane.
Wind clicks the metal leaves tonight.
I speed alive in sequence deep,
beast field rain
throbbing to the lipless pulse of windwonder.
O tormented landscape, handscape,
deathbones hewed
at my pouldrons and gorgets. Down
in the tarred and feathered department
of gutted souls the cry is so wimp: What's in it for me
but the Labour Party and geometric raisin bread?
Chomp, chomp, go the pink bleat sheep,
down to Walworth Road.
I'm such a bad and drunken lad, a fiend fellow
in the useless art of swallowing and wallowing,
as to invite brazenly her puckerage, her mayoral
addresses of correction, her buzzing network
of helplines flashing down the gorge.

Just look, I snarled my lute
in waspish worsement, claggy gob
clipped claptight shut.
I sledged it fast off my funny bondage tongue
but no one believed me above the cellar: I died
every day since I gave up poetry
and swapped it for a lake from the châteaux of France
and all of the saints – Bede, Bob, Sexton, Messrs Rotten, Johnson,
Presley and Cash – abandoned me.

Perhaps the purple plush pansies have an answer today.
Only my little yellow lanterns
spring vinelike
in their breezy Jerusalem
aiming for victory over the ordinary sunne.

Hell is the pavement against my shit face.
And the devil has seen Robert off on the bus.
The light of recovery is just a format.
The light of recovery is just a lost fairy tale
seeping with ferndamp
in the bluebell vales of your childhood.
The light of recovery is an ex-starre, furious with everlasting
darkness.

I am the addict, strapping on his monumental thirst.
The sky is livid like jigsawed lace
and there are no happy endings.

Buying Christmas Wrapping Paper On January 12

Let loose at morning from frost pockets the wind rips.
Enough to snuff blue candles in a huff of sighs.
Let's use the sensational strong stuff hanging off the wall
before we electrocute ourselves forever
to a final gleam of love. We do it like a Miró or galvanised Matisse.
Her name is Bijou, her sign The Snake.
Three-storey monsters, whipcord Judas-faced accusers and sneaks, faking
that the very sky is human
filled with sham planets, nooses not yet minted
from lunar shards
at every broken tearful opportunity
while in retarded zones
the tumblestone temple tables are turned.
Heaven's just an opened bottle
                                in a demon's argent mitts
smuggled to my unholy lips
from the squirrelled reservoir, the cached stash
in Stasi lock-ups
underneath the fallen arches
in Legless Lonnen
                down Do-lalley Drive, Kerbcrawl Boulevard, Cirrhosis Street
and Wrecked Head Road:
I am leader of the beguiled and fear of straps across my chest
cleave me to the haunted floorboard bed.
Ruthless vanity will have its day (as you know worshipped ones)
and the Stasi demons' gin-soaked bat-packed overcoats
are not different, my grave advocates, my angels, allies, brave backers and boosters,
my eternal love donors,
my decency guarantors, armpit clutch helpers
jostling to seize me in my seizures
from the cobbled gutter's facedown drenched hell,
you patrons and dauntless promoters, partners and pals,
such confrères of confidence,
my duplicate equals and ferocious friends.

Vintage and grizzled each Satan's wretch
does purl, ooze, gurgle, spurt and twirl, gyrate,
pirouette, spin, reel and swim
in grim lashing bind, unswayable elbow grease
applied to mindcrazy moonshine not hindered.
Living daily rim to mouth, rev gun throttled, quelled and jammed,
too late to stop now.

Let the dead man walk to rise is sombre fiction
my murderers will never calibrate.
                                   It and they are all upon me now
and tenebrous squalid and ignoble night
snaps its willing neck
on every lurid aspect of my rotten scowling face.

We Offer You One Third Off Plenitude

O let me plunge my feverhands into his clotted throat. Let me free
the devil's briars and combinations, even down upon my worn-out
woman's honkers, fingers hinged to wrench out infection
before it has him in the demon yard, the bad god shed, orangebox
overcoat so thinly laid.

There is more to his royal light than
wings of demon pipistrelles can dim, or dreaded Stasi hats and coats
undone to hide the starres and moon.
Busy to the last
with basin of detox vomit, I am black flag nurse, noose loosener,
penitence ring wrecker, rupture lip annihilator extraordinaire,
fierce defendress of flame faith, laver
of eclipsed kiss champ.

Revivor of the passed out poet in his pissed up plan.
In fit wrath, Notre Dame gutterspouts spring up
inside his fried lamb's liver face.

I am the woman accused: vulturefemme
pecking, beak brushing
Prometheus poisoned meat.
I am the woman admonished
with fitwords, spit bubbles
and green bad movie slime.

Yet wipe I do
to lie against him sober
when the fit has gone
and each defashioned jigsaw piece
back in place.
Yes, it is true, Albion is distressed upon her hardened knees.
The quality of mercy writ so large
upon his broken angelface.

So many darts
and drunken hurts and harms.
So many ill-formed hurtwords.
Such forays of spitting spouting guntongue.
Twelve per cent non-vintage gargoyle gurgle gobshite.

The 999 call – again.

My quivering man laid under a blue light
empty bottles left behind.

Daddy Wants To Murder Me

I write poetry at the age of seven and daddy wants to murder me.
He does a good imitation of it: beats me with a leather belt
and tears my little book in strips.
I wonder why my little poetry book, which is blue, is in strips,
and falling to the carpet like rain.
Strips and stripes, my daddy. An awesome man.
I sit in the garden reading Homer, shy lad
under a folding one-man tent and daddy wants to murder me.
Daddy, I caught a trout. Honest I did dad.
Daddy, I caught a dace away on holiday in Dorset
and it was argent like the moon when I ran, ran, I ran away
for fear of everything and you. It was argent like the moon.
It was argent daddy, but daddy wants to murder me.
Daddy, the wind murmurs and hoys against my shins
and I am alone upon my little pins in dales and hills
but my heart is chill: because daddy wants to murder me.
Daddy, do you want me to stop using the word daddy
and not write like Sylvia Plath at all?
Do you want me to write about my shrub of bay
which we can stroke on our way
out to the bender to have a hoolie and a ball? Do you daddy?
Normally, in recent literary history, daddy, it is women
who write about their daddies, daddy. But now it's me.
Daddy, da, pa, everytime I hear your name I want to flee, flee, flee.
Daddy, when the word *failure* fled into my dictionary
one page after *facetious*, I thought of you.

Words were my war weapon, no matter how much
you loved Dickens. All the names and words of endearment
I never called you, and you could never find in your dictionary
to call me, daddy, all the names of dearness, daddy, when I spat
at you in the street, and ridiculed you in public, joying at the response
to the ridicule, and my way with words as war weapons.
Daddy, when the word *hatred* sprang up in class or conversation,
daddy, you were top of the league, you were right beside the word.

And it rained.
And I love the rain, daddy, but you were never part of it.
I was out on the lawn, and it was rosy September.
Mother was addicted to wobbly eggs, and she made herself that way,
daddy, with your tremendous help. You were good at that, dad,
I give you that. Daddy, when the word *broken* fled into the
dictionary, daddy, your oleaginous self was there smiling
to give it a helping hand. Only you would have been there.

When *ostentation* fled to the hills into my upland notebook
I flaunted it right back in your direction, daddy. You knew what
it meant.

O goodness, daddy, I've dropped my dictionary,
and my knowledge of words and phrases, punctuation and properly-placed
full-stops, but I know I'm alright daddy. I can steer clear
of my stupid awfulness. You'll be there, daddy,
with a welter of words. With a punishment of punctuation.
Daddy, you personally placed the sin in syntax.

And I went to the Durham Family Practitioner Committee,
and they were very kind and told me straight, for straight
is what I need, dad, now that drink has twisted me.
One day, daddy, and this is what they said from the
bottom of their professional hearts. One day, with
rain from Sligo sheeting in the poor street, or
rain from the desolate areas of unkindly Strabane,
or from Denton Burn for that matter, or Waddington
Street, where my heart is in storage, in a furnace,
oddly enough, not in a freezer, or an ice-cube
tray (yellow, not transparent) – and don't forget
my dear da, don't ever forget. The French verb
is *oublier*, daddy – that when you sent your devil letter
your snide, sneering, you Demon With Knives In The Mouth,
daddy, when you posted it at 14:15 in the beautiful city
of Cambridge, a city that does not need your evil,
there is the letter, daddy, in the grate, where we
burned it, and when we did that, daddy, we burned you.

And when I had been to the Durham Family Practitioner Committee,
and it is housed in a marvellous building abutting the
Western Hill, and I cock my head at it always, and
when I had been to the vale, and all of the other hills
which lie in my soul, and their souls, and the souls
of all of those who have walked them and loved them
and hoped their souls and soulsongs would be collected and loved
by a poet who would always be scorned by his da, daddy.
I stood in the street at four in the day, itch of matins
and mitted palms over the river in the great cathedral.

I pondered it seemed almost forever upon the kinds
of factual annoyance you dislike, père, Mr Not Sit Him
On Your Knee, so I deliver it to you in this poem,
on my way back to the home of my great beloved, whom you
will never meet, evil devil daddy, even in the waiting room of the handsome

home of the Durham Family Practitioner Committee, who
told me, without saying one word, one verb, one sentence,
there were no subjunctive clauses or split infinitives
lying on the patients' area table, daddy, when they told me:

the rains of Sparty flower all the way from the ferry landings of
Ireland, from the land of spuds and stout, and pipes
and the great glens of poetry, Eileen Aroon and the loughs of swans
and swanning if you fancy on a very soft day, daddy. Let
me tell you how it is now – all the press releases have
been sent, and all those who received them in the world
of poetry and demons upstairs have shredded them and their faxes.
We are approaching the midday of the time of Nobody Zero, a time
of failed locks and pushed back chairs in a hurry.

It will rain, which is a day I love most, daddy. It will
pour and drip like a wound in the funny black sky. And I
will be in a badly repaired car in a field not quite the green
of the paint on at least one of the walls of the Durham
Family Practitioner Committee surgery in its handsome
building, daddy. And I think, daddy, that the car idling
on the sill of the soaking sike will be black too.
And I will hunch out of the driver seat, and
I will look at the rain and strangely enough be glad of the
rain. And this is what I learned, this is what my headwounds
and my heartstrips, and my little bookstrips were written on, pa,
da, daddy, père, this is what they told me in the red
wounds which are woven across me like very bad ribbons, daddy.

They were very reasonable, daddy, most personable,
no slyness involved, no letters unsigned posted in
Cambridge from the Headquarters of Insecure Fathers,
for that is what you are, daddy, after all, a father.
But believe me, the cheeky chappy behind you in the
miserable family photographs, you were never a father to me.
You were never a father and you were never a friend.

You saved my brother from drowning, daddy, you saved
your youngest son. O thank God, daddy. If you
can love a brother more than a brother, da, I love Paul.
Our Paul, da. But it is not enough to try and find a
redundant welder in the Durham Family Practitioner Committee
and after angry handshakes and solidarity exchanges
at the closure of another
worldwide great shipyard that I might in my poetic
unappreciated nightmare about you, daddy, ask for

flux to weld my utterly broken heart to yours in
some kind of common long lost at last agreement. I
cannot, daddy, I just cannot. The keys of my agelong
Olympia typewriter, my brilliant friend, which I carry with
me from here to there, all of those thousands of words
which I heaped against you one way or the other, for
hatred of you, or for lost love of you, and that you
never respected me for what I did.

And what they told me – and they did not know that they
had told me – in the Durham Family
Practitioner Committee, is that one day, daddy, one darkly liquid jewelled day,
I will stand

As the wind and western rain sweep from the Atlantic
into Strabane, I will bulge my shoulders, more used
to pushing open the off-licence door, bulge them
from the driver side window, all the time thinking of my beloved,
but let me tell you, daddy, what they told me, in between
the units leaflets, when I was reading them on the
badly-lit late bus going home, this is what they told me.

I would be getting out of the driver seat of the
poorly parked badly repaired car going home
in the sight of the bungalows, and they are always bungalows, daddy,
and the poorly repaired car is always black, da, it's
always black in a black spud-filled field, and always
a black day, or another Bloody Sunday, or any other
bloody bad day or month or year you dare to mention. And I will
get out of the car and I will heave my boots
across the turf and beyond the spuds, daddy,
do you remember, daddy, that's why we all left Ireland,
why we were always so envious of America, dadaddy, that's
why we were always so Popish proud, and it was raining,
belting down,
you know the rain, da, the rain we love so much, the soft rain
and the hard rain, on the rivers and hills, when we went fishing,
and it swept our very love away. And every day when we woke
it was there
as we walked up it was right in our faces.

And what they told me, was that I
will be almost half out of the black car, the Austin
A40, knee deep, god help me already, in the stricken wastes
of Crossmaglen and ugly Strabane, in the permanent borders
of crossfire, bull-horn warnings, rain-dulled crackle of

47

walkie talkies barely heard from soaking ditches, and the cross-hairs
of my heart, for this terrain, and terrain is all it is, a word with
a bleakness to it all of its own, despite a false disguise of green,
there my heart will be, steady as a drum for Billy, cold
as the kneecapping street on the outskirts, bizarre
as the surreal paintings on gable ends of those horse-riding men
in grand plumage and cockades.

Rain sheets down Hollywood-style, bigger than it is in nature.
No use hunching against it now. Collar up and the clava on and
right hand in pocket to make sure as the white-painted and pebble-dashed
bungalows worm out before me in their cheap mediocrity.
Rain their priceless diadem.

What goes through my cross-hairs heart at this time, in the final trudge,
are the beatings and berations, the betrayals of one who expected to
be loved. But then the ultimate repayment with thanks after the beltings
and verbal child abuse, when I sped up myself through sport and poetry
to be a robust youth with knockdown ideas of his own. And here was the
bungie, no more than a byre with net curtain, sidelights, bad carriage
lights, and leaden crossed porch torch as depicted on miscellaneous
false Yuletide postcards – and white oblong chime bell, which I pressed.
At least it was not Beethoven's Fifth and no dog barked: unusual.

All of that gunfire in the choke of the city, just over there. Orange
city council lights psychedelically flashed with Black and Tan
electric blue sweeps. We rocked like that in the sixties when we
fled from the various dictators and authorities. You for example, daddy.

A lad, a snow-haired cheeky chappy lad with little turned up smile
came to the door with eager I'll get it as he ran down the short hall
to the unsnecked chrome handle and yanked it in. Not more than seven,
just like the deadly sins, daddy, a wee white shirt, short pants and
Clark's sandals, eyes
still drugged with the wonders of what he had been reading in his
pocket *Aesop's Fables*. He wasn't daft at all. You could see the
awesomely distasteful glow of the red bulb imitation coal effect
from the living-room fire, and he ushered me in up the hall
the little snow-haired lad with hand outstretched inviting
me in from outside the pebble glass wind resistant door
as I felt in my pocket and asked him in a voice only loud
enough for him to hear:

Is your daddy home?

Angel Showing Lead Shot Damage

Let's dab a double finger half-pissed kiss on Muddy's lips. O
she's sixteen years old.
Tonight in the troubletorn heartland where heroes die and play,
in the knightly arenas of vainglory, demons' candle dancing
and lancing of the moon's throat will see us down
betrayed by feverfaith in love. Howl on, my pounding and delinquent soul
until her gunship
is taken up to tapers of the sunne.
Quenched ferocity, blanched faces turned indifferently
are all the twisted bee rave now.

My sleek torpedo will return, fins aflame
beneath the sheets. That's her promise.
Yet into blood I'm forged, bile and vomit
stranded in the fingers' stretch
                                    where nurses cannot come
against demonic upheavals of villainous
dread night.

Here the poet will die, pickled and puce.
Dead man walking theme tune.
Number 13 tattooed on his neck.
Beast caged behind frail and fragile bars.
So when loose
it rips the very forest to an hilarity of shreds, bones
and burns
to join her scalding kisses
just a Canon automatic click away.
She is an angel sure, a privy perle
                                    set rod-high
against all pestilence, needle and nag.
Rotten boroughs
of wine and gin
by the busload, look out!

In the land of wet brain and liver dysfunction,
subscriptions for coffin not necessary.
Messrs Demon and Sons see to everything.
And one last gargle before the screws
are twisted in.

Shreds Of Mercy/The Merest Shame

Shunned, ignored, cast off, slung in the bin,
sent from the bridge, pariah man, Mr Negative Endless,
fiercely fingered out by his ice queen and put on ice:
Gazer at photographs, kindler of memories hung on the wall.
But there's no breathing hot reality here today!
You lean, arms out east west, on the powerful rivetted
spine of our Malevich Suprematist bridge, above
the raging salmon spawning greatest river, but
it is only a picture, and the sky is moonmilk blue.

Today it's me with the twelve strings, the three
bars, me with the solo harmonica, unaccompanied
raw heart sax machine. Me with the loony frets.
No more us the boon fruits. Me Disney Dumbo big ear re-make.
Big ones, plopping pear drops splash on the silent pathways.
Always the salinations, cheek wiping, straight up
from the human salt beds. What matter this? *Don't ever leave me.*
Harmless nightdressed Palladium utterance
it really seems. Yet it blows like thunder
crushing at least one fucked up skull.
When it pops out of my enzyme count I'll sign for it,
if write I may and can. Don't bank on it, as in bank.

My great hero Kazimir Malevich, how the moon the other night
was just like your Suprematist plate in 1917, when
you quietly stormed the waiting world
with your railway sidings. I wear a cap in honour of you.
Now I have my CAFE CUBANO – Tueste Oscuro, and
today, with the rosemary flowers so azure
beneath the borage heavens, I,
like you, and Sergei and Vladimir, hate
all of my replicant oppressors, double-breasted
faces, Otis lift tunes all of the way to the boardroom if you fancy.
And Kazimir, I think of your wonderful plate, wonderful
is not too great a word to use. Indeed, it is undervalued
these very salination days, these days of liver expansion.
And Sergei, and Vladimir, I think of your guns,
and what they can eventually do. I used to myself shoot one,
but never at myself, though I have always had reason.

Yes, bless, blessure, bliss and blood, worst and wine
are my saintly, thorny words. I am crowned by them!
Not wearing fur-fringed gloves upon her flinty fingers

which sometimes taxed my shifting planets, she
felt my collar, for I am a drunken criminal of overspent
love, and she threw me in the jail of my terrible life.
Always in the locker of my single-minded lit-stricken cuffs
reaching for the emerald glass cylinder
cork within aperture, and the demons rampant
in their crest cockiness hands down my throat.
Hysterical psychotic drain cleansers.

In With The Stasi

Gnashed fervour licks down like fire
as the diazapam takes over and I lurch worse than drunk
down the locked ward. Barred windows, bedlam,
and all that mashed potato. I am mashed
also, stale holocaust bread without milk.

The autumn leaf which blows its tiny way
through the wonderful universe
before streams sweep it into nowhere.

No milk, just water with the dosage, urine. No wine.
But that is the curse of the Demon who shall always
be known as The One With the Mouth filled
with Rustling, Restless and Relentless Blades.
The wine comes complete with salt! Drink
at your own expense, but lap that brine. Suck
the Dead Sea dry and imagine it best burgundy.

In the hospital, locked and barred in the Harding Ward,
up the redbrown carpet into the first floor mental asylum,
away from the ground floor ward of patients under section,
with a blue carpet, with a phone, as in telephone, booth
working, first charge 20p, 10p not enough, 10p to
the red telephone company and 10p to the new trust,
which frankly seemed minimal, even the most heroic
twig of my family's tree died for want of mashed spuds
in Cork on the blanket on a prison bedbunk, it's all
on the gravy train of pills down the dry throat
and the mashed taties a comforting white collar.

I was not there to hold his hand when he died for
freedom and he was not in bedroom 4 to hold mine
when very funny vermilion lines slide viper-like
up the wall escaping the ant-gangs gathering to
plan a throat-choke raid on me at 4.50am.

Knocked up at 7 for the showers, the brain-dumbing
first knock-out of the day, the tick-off from Mr Starched
White Coat with Himmler clipboard, then the shit-brown
bran after a look at the slumped pink cardies to see
if death had come upon them yet. We tumble to
The Trough and exchange our troubles. And when we,

except Tony, dying from self-imposed malnutrition
and not from any kind of certifiable brain disease,
and who was from a village sacked by the shock troops
of this present Government, and not even on a proper
glucose drip, sitting on his bed in Bedroom Four, and
when we, not to repeat to even test your listening boredom,
sank back pill-brained and detoxing into bed, I
knew why in 1994 the windows were still iron-barred.
No corpses to be found on the York stone flags please
or it would have meant deducted funds on April Fools Day.

Pasolini Demon Memo

The Jesus Christ Almighty is a barely stripling bare-chested biker.
Bolting Pharisee jailers shaking shackles and chains, knuckled
love and *hate* in Galilee blue, ace of clubs across his tanned blades.
He rides into town on a Vincent Black Shadow and moves his feet around.
My territory, his territory.
But we won't fight it out. We won't do a Hemingway.
We'll exchange bike parts, accelerating road stories
and little-known facts about best oil and chrome polish.
In our eyes we can both see it: no curses or cures, both
on a dustbowl highway leading to the cleansing of temples
and the unstrapping of my Goliath gargle gargantuan addiction.
He had telling things to say and I had mine. Townsfolk
arced around in an awe of wariness and dread, planning
all mock trials ahead.
He had a cross to go to
and I have mine.
O yes, let's kick some Makem Pharisee
scruffs from the thrash-hot main drag
handing in all badges and spreading allegiance to nobody.
Together let's beat the smotherers of justice.
Fill her up, load her up, ready to run.
Your blood's fluxed with serious innocence and grace,
but my tongue tells me I need something stronger.

Ferocity?
Try me my provoked and peppery friend.
Meanwhile, until the thunder rolls
and the street becomes a bloodbath,
come inside and lean against the bar.
Red wine for you, gin for me,
as the menfolk shrink away.

Later we'll listen to the eternal music of plovers.
You'll meet Pearl and her unremitting ceaseless silence.

I'll tie one on, ready for a vomit seizure
alone in the treeline.
Expecting an overcooked cauliflower brain
convulsion, a horizontal twitch dance in the locoweed.
Addicted to alcohol, poet away with the prairie fairies,
the monkeys and the demon mixer.

Ignore me and the medics arriving
stuffing the bottle down a gopher hole.
Stick around.
You'll make sheriff one day.

Nil By Mouth: The Tongue Poem

Demons, big-hatted and hard-hatted, far as gutter-toppled
squint-eye with grapple-lost spectacles can see, custard brain
head slanty on kerbside perch, vomit ready for a roller ride
into the X-rated, dog arse emptying unlit street, mongrel eyeing
the demon conveyors from here to eternity, bottle after bottle,
twisted cork to twisted head and unscrewed, screwed-up life,
over the slag heap of stonegrey aggregate from the moony saltpan
beds where the stones will surely lie upon my swollen liver,
as the swollen argent river sweeps across the tumblestones.
Grog demon biceps leaving me moan groggy, foggy-bonced,
pouring lunarstruck salt, sel de mer, coarse white pellets
scuttle-funnelled on MacSweeney's stuck-out begging tongue:

Tongue stuck out like raw begging hand in the mall, sticking
out straight, single digit filthy message signal up yours tongue,
in the air bloated for booze upright needle Cenotaph tongue,
grovelling, whining, soliciting, pleading, eyes imploring,
thirst, thirst, thirst, craveache, pinecovet, itchneedlust,
but on comes the salinating, saliva-droughting insult, Sahara
mouth an agony O, my Lot's wife tongue, rough orange fur tongue,
tongue examined by Dr Guo in needle room number two,
bladderwrack tongue late of the ebbingtide pools, salt on the rocks,
tongue of the deep sea trawler lick hull clean department,
tongue out on rent as a dog's public park hard-on, for
artists to paint in glory of its pinky stiffness and quality
as blotting paper for anything as long as it's a double on the rocks.

Blot, blot, blot, blotting me out: moan, moan, take me
from the slake tide to lake or snaky clean river, before
the endless chained pails of salt end me, tireless demons
happy in their work: a regular seven dwarfs scenario,
whistling darkly all the way to the daily saltbeds as
they pour, pour, pour, and the demons' capped gaffer,
fancy Dan Demon Man, who shall always be known as
the one with the Mouth of Rustling and Relentless Blades,
swaggers barely into focus from my throne in the gutter,
one hand filled with bottles and the other with scran.

Just one more, sir, for the road?

Demons In My Pocket

Arrest me asleep, crashed out
under the eye of the borage: So what? I'm
just pissed as a primrose posy
beneath an April shower. I'll do.

At least I'm speaking in cogent sentences
from the back of nowhere below an argent moon.
At least I'm not a replicant Labour Party goon.
I sold my fancy suits for vodka and a copy

of The Russian Experiment in Art.
It was the only way I could get near
Kazimir. I stood proud alone
in the Stalingrad rain and read

the legend headlines: Fiend Poet
Shot Dead With Broken Hat. Scald
Of The Steppes Before Firing Squad
Accused Of Dawdling On Lithic Tuff

With Shattered Socialist Heart – Gun
Seized. Friend Of Few Flees Not So
Lengthy Life With Unpunished Book.
But they were all too long or badly

bust and the typeface choice at least
debatable. So much in my oddly spring-
like foreign guises – Swanne, Ludlunatic,
MoonySwooney, Madstag, Lenin Wolfboy or

swiftly skilful terrace tantalising
push and run teaser fan pleaser Sweeno –
I yearned for 200-point Cyrillic caps
across seven cols or in cirrus strands

and to be a bloodred flower too, guts &
heart upon my sleeves and not a pinko posy!
Not to be out in rainy Nevsky Prospekt
but here I am at the back of nowhere

under a fickle sickle harvest five-year
plan pearly Shirley shiny moon, dreaming
in my railway sidings way of tiny toes
and teeming tumblestones twined without

torment in greeny locks and coronets
of cushy crushed footfall meadow cowslips. In
the dimmed and dimming day when it
will be dark along the river and always

dark and Othello will pad freely demented
a panther in my sickened heart, I feel
the gutter twisting, hard-fortuned
carrier of water and nitrates to the

unholy earth, and it all, all, yes, all
of it, howls in the basement bowels as
the gale gets up its fatal goat. Starlings
thrash the sky at dawn in feathered

shoals, quitting nightrest rooftop
cat-free safety of the city centre Odeon.
Truly, I do have 20/20 Vision: She's
gone, she's gone, but what can I do? What

drives me to you is what drives me
insane. Mental rental idiots in hatred
uniform pursue me through fire
escapes to arrest once and forever

before the racing sails of my heart
can capture her eyes of borage blue.
They'll drag me away from B&Q the
gall and spite and malice crew, to

filthy demon paperwork and drinkwork,
to slurword work, collapse hardwork,
to tonguebite drudgery *grand mal* jerkwork
and far away, my fingerfast, from you.

All my rotten reeking shrieking shreds
are speaking fast now, sledging off my
funnybone tongue. The very last words
sung, they're exploding and expanding

as they hit the croaking creaking rhizome
rats' tail ground. Outbreak! Outbreak!
Thousands dying and thousands dead! It's
more an incurable curse than a human

tempest clashing in the midnight blue
of the outer outskirts of Murmansk.
All human malevolence planned, sewerage,
invade my hair and lips and lovely

blue far horizon cloud cotton-soft eyes.
Killer virus in my brain bane, this liquid
poison potion passion pestilence for which
I have shown so little prayerful penitence

coughs its infection into my lovely kitten
drunken face. Spikes, brads, studs and welds
bussed up the bombed-out road from Nixville
to empty eager waiting bottle-holding hands.

Nailbite squall-stirring helicopter gunships
of darkest green – it is dark now along the
moonless river and dark and always dark –
descend to drop the flogging hammers in.

Tell Anne she can have her wildest pills
again tonight and the devil be on look-out.
My rattlechain hands go out unshaking now
in feverfew frenzy, big Russian tarragon

twister tornado as it whips its Monroe hips,
in the hostile thunder bellow days alone away
from you my lovegun, my bullet to the heart.
The violence universal of all you warders,

white coats or blue: needle room number two,
Chinese doctor grinning at me Manchurian
Candidate with her needles and punctures,
bars or no bars, mashed spuds or no spuds.

In single mode I speak out clearly astride
the argent turquoise starre system which
beams in your eyes. No log-in further
sequence needed. To log-out now means to die.

And the terrible gutters move again aching
with gargoyle gushing rain above the graves
dug by those who will lie in them horizontal.
The moon's awesome gaping craters lean in

and the lurid savage cranberry sunne muscles
up inside its squadron of burning over and above
the iceblue rims of the fabulous fjords. Is that
Kazimir, John or Percy in the railway sidings

astride or in or beneath or moving through
the water? It is the streaming dark water,
for the water is dark and it is always dark
and the night is dark and cold is the very ground.

The emerging lanceheads of the chives are so
beautiful tonight, by offshore rigs, mainland
bridges and cranes, and humans walk beneath
the stars by the streaming dark water where

in the land of tumblestones it is dark and always
dark. Hear the roots of the flowers stress even
the mighty earth and cry. Feel the mad planet
buckle at the soul and knees. This memo to all:

I am 72-inches tall, yet when I go to meet John
and Percy and Kazimir and Pearl, stick me in
an oven and burn me just the same. Then I will
be a true Jew, a poet through and through.

The Horror

The horror of the hospital for us both.
Demolished eager hopes and trudges up the bad
steep hill in your dun winter clothes: to be
refused information. Not your bright red
party jacket not your guitar badge and
funny pinned on chrome figure. Just
petitions and pleas – how's that man
of mine? That badly displaced fellow
on 50 mils a day and what, what for
god's sake, is he eating, and I don't even
believe in gods – or that one from
Cecil B. De Mille. For when the Wall,
and I don't mean the tourist attraction
touted in China, when the Wall was
chipped to bits it broke my stern heart
and it broke his, my man, and I know
you are breaking his and mine now.

And you are breaking me to uphill
trudge bits and episodes – like poor
hammered toffee – and I cannot eat
myself and I am being distracted
my heart itself once an oven of love
turned into a rainy asylum alone
in the bleak upland rains. How
much better it might be in summer,
recovering our seasons released
upon sensational sun-peeled skin,
boats and oars and oarlocks and
handlocks and kisslocks locked
right in place, pure juice from
Spanish oranges, Miró suns pouring
endless light over grief of my walk
across the spated river, touching
the black painted bridge lamp after
dark, made in Brum, near where
Nazi airmen torched my childhood
cathedral; me in a shelter, afraid
of flames and fire, as you are now,
flames in your heart, O darling
don't let them be extinguished now,
it is the smashed cathedral of your
life sweeping up in utter flames

to the frozen ground: torched and
charged with terrible destruction.

For many days, my man, you were
a man with a many-layered mask.
You did not want to know me and
again as I arrived and arrived you
bent your head and heart away and
did not want to know me. My own
heart a haunted husk without you.
But always I put my hand out and
want to and always did and do. We
have been driven to distractions
by a long revelation of deprivation
madness which triggered me to
trudging, loving you, pursed lips
grim in every worried step back
to your haloed bed in wardlight.

Your northern arms around me
not browned by Miró's molten suns,
and you held me strong and lovingly,
northern hands, tight, tight, tight,
forearms around my ribs and spine,
making me shudder in happiness
and unbroken realms of loving safety,
so paleness of spirit left me undaunted;
a queen of hearts and a warrior of love!

Yet once more I am at the hospital door.
Once more you will be completely
off-centre and pilled up, caustic tongue
not lazy. Once more betraying my heart
your illness clinging like oak-roots.
I pray the trees will lend you strength.
The time has come to palm aside all
images of lost sheep and willows weeping.
In my bad dream you climbed to the wet
roof of the lunatic asylum, through barred
windows, determined to be demon free.
You said you were a magpie and would
fly to me. But your flight ended in a fatal
swan-dive into the Yorkstone yard. O
mendacious reel of bad fortune, let
sun's pollen-gold wake me to a saner world
so fleet already without this torment too.

Demons Swarm Upon Our Man And Tell The World He's Lost

Smartism seems to be the best deal
in these broken-fire days, honed up
with barely held apologies, not the
Suprematism of monumental Kazimir.
He'd weep seven broken plates at its
purity of abjectness, lack of muscle
tone. Not for us now to stand upon
the steps in a revolution's moment,
with Miró's crown of sun and stars.

All the demonic graffiti is quite certain:
     I'm the abjuring man.
     I'm the abdicating man.
     I'm the strangely dislocated
     disconnecting disconnected man.
     I'm the storm-tossed tosser
     on Earthquake Street, mindblown
     dead on arrival sprawled on
     Richter Scale Prospekt, found
     crying wolf beside the troikas.
     I alone in detox itch and fury
     test the temper of sunbeams
     and angels. I flee across the shiny
      floor – believe me, it is shiny –
     headbackward pursued by flying
      animals and objects each
       with forktail cocktail blazing. Endless anger
       only is my recompense for
        first-rate pistolage now she's
       fled these shores for sanity.

     O my wires keep dropping out.
     Let loose my stumble in the darkness.
     Fling my face into brooding earth.
     Trample forward onto footloose ground.
     Watch the devil's tarpit veil smother me.
     Who today will fetch my idle drinkless
    hands a king whose neck wants wringing?
     Who will set me free from strapdown
     to deliver Sexton's necessary utmosts?
      It will be the last house-call after all.
      No, no, it is all drinkless dole and drollery,
     regime of hysterical tomfoolery.

Why can't you get helium on the National Health?
Because the Tory Government has taken it all.
It is dispensed every day to Cabinet ministers.
Now they are gone completely myxomatosis bunny funny.
May the demons track them down
as they tracked me. Relentless pursuit
and capture their family's fantastic method
code and motto. O, SAS where are you now?
Gone to an alcohol oasis every one.
Blackhand gangs through every window
leapt craving my wit from ice-wagons – every day
was Drink More Pour More Day.
May they sting their heads and hearts
and sap their very strength and breath.
Am I alone in my symmetrical vision
of this unequivocal stupidity? Look
at the Labour Party too & roar with laughter.
All, all, all, clowns of conceit.

Shafted & driven intolerant on spewground
wearing only an orange Cuba baseball cap
say then this: Lift one much exercised
right arm more used to shifting Russian
vodka, drunkenly saluting naked and badly
bruised Albion and that failure St George,
declaring in soaking mattress rawness –
that's the ugly nation you have made.

And that's the nation of me too: each of us
in very separate parts brought to our knees.

Hooray Demons Salute The Forever Lost Parliament Of Barry And Jacqueline

Now it is time to put aside and forget
the decadent period of fast red cars &
slothful attitudes towards boldness
and moral mettle except in entering
the National Lottery, the greatest
con yet wrought by the Tory Party –
worse than cheap gin for quelling
here in the Great United Quelldom
where tomorrow never comes fast
enough for win ticket announcement.

I have been admiring the caked
menstruation blood you left
on a pillow before we parted.
It was the most tender
moments of our days.
We laved and laved the blood away
and you helped me with my broken leg.
It's amazing what we did considering.

Nothing remains now.
World in smithereens.
4:56, sun rising after me,
swoon alone in the garden
at lilac and azalea fumes
thanking heaven inside
the utter madness for
nasturtium you planted
before fleeing from
my darkriver drinking.

Rain, alone in the rain,
rain and the train and
the river darkly summoning
towards its source my heart.
All the buttercoppes
flush like forests ankle-high.
I am so glad to live at the
northern end of the earth!

The south would suffocate
and humiliate me. Once more
the blossoms and birds. Even
aconite and horehound
bloom and bloom. I&I

myself am in a poisoned
corner, Chatterton-style,
entirely deconstructed.
Toe pressing the mad earth.
Stiff bottom lip turned out
against the rules and rest
of it, all in despotic shame.

Said: should do, but I won't.
And she said: that's the story
of your life. Almost man.

When The Candles Were Lit

Rain, rain, rain again and bonerolling bloodthunder,
    lampblack clouds from the Pennines
        towards fjords in the east
          releasing their load
    soaking the tied-back crown of Russian tarragon, swaying
        so high in the herb garden
         – reminding me
of the cast-back hair of Anne de Bretagne in 1514
commemorated in marble: full-length along the sealed casket
eyes closed by human hand, lips half-parted for a last kiss,

    O please, O please beloved,

    and those frontal bones and ribs pushed up
    made more emphatic in her exit exhalations
      in the Cathedrale Basilique Saint-Denis
        as the young beauty
        longed to find her breath.

    Yes, Paris, you have everything,
    the fastest nitrate in the best Laforgue rain,
    the best gutters and downpipes and poets
and the marble hightide hair swept back in death pose
      like wind-whipped tarragon.

Pearl Against The Barbed Wire

How sweet today the scents and air perfumes
down the overgrown flags, binding stems
cling to my fair descending legs
which never saw a proper dance
in the arms of another — at village gatherings
I could only nod, neither saying
yes or no. So charmless harmless me!

Yet the true blue cranesbill like heaven's light, invading
our brilliant path at Sipton Shield, crowning
the riverbed of tumblestones, is my
queenly ankletwine today, and the Michaelmas
which will be for my hair, washed
in the white water, crown of hair
lashed back from my supple neck, O yes
I hoy it back, defiant almost, if I knew
the word defiant and I wished I did know,
for it is a gunmetal word with a hard 't'
all should be acquainted with, with which all
should be in talking agreement: talking, what's that
my sky-blue eyed Bar?
You speak the petals off the trees
each day and I in wonder
watch you draw them down. You're like a bird
with fluting beak, while the silence
of the Nenthead shafts populate
with lack of noisesomeness my full
disabled cleft and tongue.

To call me idiot, brand me nobody,
is bestowing lustrous ermine qualities
upon my nowhere frame. There are no proper words for me.

Pearl: now our secret paths above the tumblestones
are pierced by yellow arrow marks
for all of those who would walk there too.

Everybody's tortured, everyone's in chains.

I hate them and loathe them with strengthening abundance,
forehead-strong, and when my abundance, my overflowing
emotion, my abundance of the heart, my
moorland affluence and wealth which others call poverty,

when it streams like a fire seam,
I loathe them for binding my pearly toes.

I hate them because I am among their
other refugees. They put up the wire, wire, wire,
along my way,
which no one should do, for wire
is an industry, a containment, made in
Leeds or Wakefield Bar said, brought by 12-wheeled lorries
in unrolled bales like silver hay
from some industrial graveskin graveyard
completely contrary to the wings of my spirit.

Fraught I am with poor lip service,
destroyed and betrayed
and the river flows from me, my molten white water,
1500 to 1400 to 1300
                          past hawhips and sloes
and so to the sea.
I will wash myself in it forever.
Darling, reader and writer with azure eyes,
eyes the colour of the sea's horizon,
I will wash myself in it forever.

In umber spate it ripped my breastbuttons, like your eager hands.
It broke apart my loving heart, like your cruel talking lips.
It stopped my sense.

O love, in a world of shuffled papers
and cheap haircuts, your honeysuckle-
scented locks, your locked and gripped
tongue will always be delight to me. In
an alien world of distant characters,
you'll always be inside the dangerous
part of my forever welling willing heart.

Bar, Bar, barbed wire. Bar, the barbs
and staples and hooks and eyes. Did
you see the photographs? Did you see
the charred skin, the gravedigging
ceremony with gleaming boots,
spectacles and sneery smiles?

Did you take note my angel poet
of the complete famine due to
circumstances beyond control
of let's grin and bear it?

Did you see the bushels of knees
and other thinly-appointed limbs
and the gaps of extracted – there's
a word, my Bar, I know you'd love –
teeth, did you wonder where the world
was, where the world went, my honeysuckle love?
Blonde but a Jewess just the same.
No one had our words in those days.

When we stared and wandered
and stored and wondered
in each others' far-reaching eyes

beneath the croaking creaking tumblestones
where our trout leapt mad for midge and mayfly
pollen puffed in gold explosions by sucking bees,

our ankles smoothed to Oriental beauty, before
either of us knew where was the Orient, before
Jeremy travelled there, before you read me

Fu-Manchu and the Yellow Peril, O dimmer
of my heavy lids, dizzy with pollen and sunlit
prose, O stunning quiet reader, seducer

of pathside petals and birdy wings, bringer
of betony, pointer out of fairies' chimneys,
runner of rings in the rinsing rain.

I stood in any light there was, in
every light, dark and almost dark,
fiercely black, like a dark heart torment,
strangely grey all the way all day
from the storm-shaken ferry jetties of Ireland,
and I stood there, arms, heart and mouth open,
ready to be annoyed and poorly-addressed
by the sudden sun over the longing of the law,
and ready to be addressed by my loving love.

Medici? Three syllables, my honeysuckle
tumblestone rosehip love, but I did not
feel like an Italian court princess, for
my vowels were uncut marble then.

Even writing the words *rose* and *garment*
broke my heart; their real variousnesses
pricked me awake when I expected it least.

O my love, my rosehip plucking love, my love,
kiss the bandage from my face and haul me from the wire.

All the mam-made hems, the man-made hymns,
none of the blood-filled truths, none, I say none,

none of them can move or call me as you can.
O my love, my harping, high fell honeysuckle

tumblestone molten white water love, haul me
from the terrible terror of the wristblood wire.

Nothing Are These Times

I am gnawing jawface, furman, odd cove
alone in the tree-line, pawpoison back
of the track pack, blood beneath the rolling

mills of sense, MC for this mad filthy earth
whose prancing demon gaffers have me
straight between the shoulder blades

and down the garglevomit hole they call
a throat. I am the bloatstoat, floating
volevoter at the collapse pollstation.

Each bouncer's waistcoat gemstarred
with fragments of Bunting Betelgeuse.
Utterly I say in the dark and demon cup:

was it not brokenwing swanlove on
the rocks which left us forlornly grieving?
Do parts of your brain go guavapulp?

Or do you just become another child-
belting father and repeat the mistake?
Does hand-wringing become a new habit?

Fierce broken light arrives in the sky
shaded by a linen shawl of Irish winds:
beating demon daddies for once seem far away.

All gulpdragons have me by the breath
& my broken heart a wretched drumbeat
now you have swanned aloft in his arms.

Sleepless nights, stalk fever in my shoes.
Bad crack, smack, nerve gas and Tarzanjuice.
Pharoah's army nurses come right in

smiling like the greetings card Jesus
in the fairytales. We're their broken bread,
their human weeds, not flowers on

the pearly path to Jerusalem. If it isn't
up the nose, it's down the head-drain
or in the skin. Anyway it's death & death's

delay button with shaky finger on it.
And we're here in the eternal land
of sensible branflake breakfasts

with UHT crap semi-skimmed clarts
from France. We hated it even more
than we loathed ourselves, each nailed

to the fantastic frantic demon tree.
Yes, it's the best the council can manage
and it's a bright hole and nothing at all.

Friends, fellow non-members of the
black sun anarchist nada addict group:
we're in for a lousy final chapter.

No end in sight in starry bruisy night.
Bad bus one way to Snowville.
Forgiveness sold out no longer available.

Dead Man's Handle
(after a word by Mayakovsky)

Comb the crawling morning chill chilling sky in search for vodkafire.
Forgive me my combing, forgive me my crawling, forgive me my fire.
The blue sky, the blue cold sky.
Forgive me, forgive me, forgive me, my kisses now lost opportunity.
Forgive me for the cold blue sky painted in your eyes.
Forgive my knee-bending
when I pleaded with you to forgive me, forgive me,
transforming your face into a planet for kisses, forgive me my lipkeen leaning.
The spangled sky with no gods in it, forgive me for not giving you gods
and the very moon a humble eye reflecting our folly, forgive me my folly
as we walk here in the windstrewn gravity defence league posture department
destroying all that is dearest
all that is best to already broken hearts. Forgive me my heart,
my clownhearted tidal wave heart, forgive me my heart.
Picasso's peace dove just a pullet with broken craw,
dead olive twigs choking its throat. Not even worth eating, forgive me its
breaking.
The whole world a cubist disaster waiting to happen.
That cracker Jack crept in and killed the begonias with his winter switchblade,
forgive me his knife-edge.

Christmas is here and there'll be no summer.
Tomorrow really has arrived already and there'll be no today.
We walk apart in the night
and it may as well be continents
disproving history
that swannes mate for life.
It's no life but a blank sheet again, all watercolours washed out in the rain
which was our growing season. Rainbow even
& soup by a lake.

Now it's dreadful and filled with dread.
Forgive me the black city which burns in my heart.
Listen to the crashing windows from the burning black cathedral,
the blazing jetblack cathedral of my broken heart.

Here comes the dazzling darza drinks-at-the ready
DEMONSPIEL:

the trophy is poisoned
electric blue
all manners gone from the window

Go then, go back, go back to the halls of hell
go back to the single toll of the bell
go back, return, turn back to the empty bed
or the bed a linen scrapheap shaken by illusory sex for one miserable night only
then the deft departure at dawn, sly handsome fish through the net, the weeping,
the illusion
of coherence
the dream of integration
all the tables in the halls of hell

alive with broken jigsaws,
fragments, pieces, worse than Paddy's Market, heart ripped out again
sad in its bowing, alone in its screaming & dreaming

driven from heaven, screwed down and abandoned
in the windswept yawning tunnels within the halls of hell

go then, to your pillow of nails,
go then, to your coldfeet unmatched boats
go then, no ruddy waterfall of leaves on our tree
go then, sober & seeing everything so damned Warwickshire clearly
go then, to the solo crystal vision of yourself

These 252 mile an hour headlong thoughts towards the station and platform
at the final appearance of the jammed dead man's handle:

Always
gutterbright
to sky's light

the eternal gift
of starres

last train to Demonville right on time.

Himself Bright Starre Northern Within
(for J.H. Prynne)

There is absolutely no record
of goodness in the history of my soul.

I say delete world delete her dollypops,
delete great gulp Adam's apple Eveorange
delete all fancy her fingers throat-gripping
delete four winds sixteen windows
delete all the sad memories the torn books daddy
delete he with belt and Charlie Dickens
in his own privately-owned bad big Bleak House.
My house in the great city, my heart, my single solo
overture, over to the lightning-begging trees.
Delete memories, no memory for them
scattered, only one execution, not enough:
we did not cleanse
we did not feed the greenwood tree.
We flew aloft naked, one second only
not trusting the present: delete
the whole future dolldoodle dollywobble,
breastbabe delete dalliance Sun Alliance.

Dance dancing in the street delete
delete mugshots handcuffs social work aftercare
all known germs in cell fungus caught on spider carcase –
delete persons unknown teeth taken
spectacles and shoes piled high to the sky

delete all bank records of Nazi gold

delete the Swiss
and Zurich accountants
delete client confidentiality: we won't tell you who went
to the ovens
               who sank beneath the brainbullet, the pointed Luger
at wrist's interface delete delete

the JUDEN window the smashed starre

delete the flogged animal
alone in byre's blackness
delete the gas through ten shower holes
delete the savaged champion horse

76

delete the wordstation *forgiveness*
to be logged in by a nobody person not one
delete

I say delete midnight, midnight lawstarres, Pearlwords,
the mojo moon, no executed kings tonight, never enough,
delete kisses, poutlips, fast breasts, all the once-couple talk.

Ban delete all big skies Northumberland Texas to Samarkand.
All soft mouths, no salmon facedown in the pools, poisoned wraps
& wrappettes, down my legs in the tumbledown lone stones.

Forever. Delete all stolen slate from Nichol's byre nail fingers,
no fashion book available, no delete kisses button. Press it.
Delete all beautiful hand-made stone walls. All wonderful swanne quillpens.

Jibesneers, delete, citric fake mouths, sad eyes masking
erection false pledges and bounced vows, refer to drawer.
Extracted teeth with no anaesthetic. Then to the ovens,

just like a book or Jew. Publisher it was thee, you.
Delete longing I will not long for her up in the tree-line. Delete plaid
woven Tunisian brought-home blankets I will not lay a bed for her.

She reversed me my heart, she deleted me in very bad favour.
Delete sunne I won't smile in it the photographed poet upland bonny
lad. Never. I will not I won't I won't ache especially for her.

She's a distant thing. It's a special promise – I won't ache for her.
Each daw dawn in the argent slipstream I lie alone I won't ache for her.
When Mars goes to bed and I lie on my left side I won't miss her a forlorn
trance of Germany starres, I'll kill my lips for telling lies.
Delete Parliament, delete pushiest pout, delete plover west window.

Paul Celan, Paul Celan, Paul Celan, Paul Celan, nothing left to bruise.
Did you see the ovens, did you smell the awesome awful gas?

I was in the so-called shower and it rained right down on me.
I was so impressed I almost goose-stepped my way to the very front.

Delete all swinging wands of the wild fell rose, no more headlong chases

stalking the pearl moon which tonight is a broken opal crescent
delete all clocks put back at midnight in the soaring pouring rain

delete A1 crash victim Catherine through Land Rover windscreen
dead on arrival Morpeth wrapped in steel & glass after Wagner concert

delete her roadside brains long camelhair coat long late bus smiles
her fast clicking shoe heels speeded and rinsed with Northern rain

delete her forever lingering grin soon to be ruined & smashed completely
facedown in a lay-by body crushed and crumpled like Christmas paper

delete rain on the border at Hawick, delete beautiful rain in Glasgow
delete the soft water of Scotland, the proud taps, brilliance everywhere

clean drops dazzle off the cone-ends, off the sleeve-catching branches
how eyeful it all is up here in the uplands, delete all nonsense, delete good sense

proper behaviour delete upstanding citizen, terminate, erase, abolish,
abrogate, annihilate, very late, annul, cancel, cease, destroy, efface,

excise, negate, obliterate, literally omit, so close to vomit, one letter only.

Our eyelashes flicked silently and closed together down the middle of
Platform Two. I was a rich entrancing beast fulled with rampant bloode.

Hands, four of them, delete. Please dad I'm only seven don't hit me.

Stop beating me over the head. All I wanted was to write a poem, I
really don't know why. It just came to your son a lad in the windrow,

out of the snowfells out of the badly described sky. I know I'm an uphill
wanderer, a poor citizen, a republic of tents, springwater my fancy & Pearl.

See how I delight in it, you're so disappointed daddy that you cannot
control me. That, even at seven, is my eternal wish. My biggest dish.

Look where we walk up a height & raining & the flame-tipped trees.
Delete the chough the lark in the fastcut meadow.

Beware me in thunder.

Look at the buttercoppes down in the meadowbank, so yellow
as I look again into my craving craven heart. I'm the hound inside

your head, the suddenly-stiffening corpse in your bed, the long and lengthy
beads of dread, right up here in the heather-glad Highlands, my lands,

I will walk where the plover walks. Hold to it, stick to it. Be faithful
to the very cause. I will forever be the Silver Shadow, the grey shadow

standing tall & silent alone in the gardens beneath a silky opal moone.
This severe thing, hard time knowing, delete hard time, sounds like Dickens,

just a note penned in darkness, darling, trying to delete this severe thing,
trying to replace the whole complete person, the whole complete poem.

I will never ever wear three hats in one day ever again. Had hair then.
Delete reality and endless punishment, O Daddy please don't beat me.

I'll be as big as Charlie Dickens one day in my big lonely Elvis Orbison heart.
I was quite alone in ruthless daylight, fastly sinking under an argent moone.

Upcoming I saw the sunne, saw the light of heaven in a toilet roll.
I looked at the yellow toilet roll – thinking it the sunne – & beheld its gaze.

What happened to my incredible fantastic endless lovely fargone literacy?
All you end up with is Pound's petals on a wet black bough. Two lines.

Delete. Beware, beware, the shredded torn paper of the silver starres.
Delete all Pearls, beware, the cat's in the bag and the bag's in the river.

Emily your crystal vision – the Soul has bandaged moments –
delete the bite the ever-holding smitten grip, between your tongue & discreet lips:

You yourself bright starre, unbroken in the petty fetters,
delete her hairbun, when will you come in with Anne Sexton

to see if I'm still alive? I'm depending on both or either of you.
Listen Em: I like your solitude. Anne is drunk like me & far too rude

and useless unreliable. She's in bed too late. Drugs, drink, mad sex.
One of you betrayed everyone, not you Em with your cheeky sparklespecks.

It's just not you: it's more New York than New England.

Where in heaven is my timeless bride?
Where is she in her beautiful glide

to the frozen bathroom at 3 in summer
at 7am in the falling January snow?

I'll lie there alone and never, never know.
Pang in the mouth I am terrified of Ireland,

more so than the broken-down collapse of England,
because in the Republic Finnbar would be found out

for what he is. Guzzler, collector of demons, bar
snaker, Baggot Street crawler, hater of Poseurs.

Three bubbles in the glass of Jesus juice,
every single glass, Aislinn, one more after the other.

I stood on the edge of the world once, not caring,
there was a woman in white before my eyes went black.

Before my hurrying down throat became swollen & bruised.
I'll never be your flame. I'll never be your flame in a bush.

Ash, I am thoroughly poisoned, and no amount of
endless Parisian beauty can resurrect me to the stand-up station.

There was a six-feet man delete with a single silver argent starre.
He cast a long black shadow, high-heeled, & unfortunately, it was me.

O Tammy, I am but a fake *prince*, no horse, I stride all tall alone.
Only the demons come to me at dawn and say in unison: you'll be bonny once
again one day.

Delete the brightbairn, the laughing lad, the happy son, the singer of songs,
the larker out-larking the breast-high larks, out in the mad spring meadow.

Delete being under the hellhounds' paws, padding over thee,
right on your chestbreast, think yourself an upright man do you?

I've always believed I stood on the earth blessed with angel wings.
Even when I slurred terribly, mad with drink, my tongue was straight.

Delete fast pastures, hound hound alone with the pack,
hound with his vixen, and the endless need to attack.

Angel hound wings, hellhound hymns, no matter how many, no matter how
many, no matter how many, I will never like Sexton row to God,
I am alone with the pack on the frozen bypass without a wincing jade.

Houndangel wings, out of the sunne, and into northern starres,
hanging up your axe most prettily, O Em don't tongue-flay me!

Enemies say starchy but I say crispness & always tell the absolute.
You'll hide in my armlock, gently, for I am a passion prince.

Passion has always been me, even before my swollen drunken days.

Raw and savage and notwithstanding passion, all of me, all, all,
swanne on the misty lake to the very end of my days. Dark, willing

on my starre charger, high on the law, up on the fell, hear that
very single solo bell, by a fastly moving running river and under a completely
useless rainbow.

Anne Sexton Blues

I

Woke up this morning
        in Newcastle Wyoming
Atlanta Northumberland
on the glory grain plateaux of Texas
Anne Sexton all around my bed.

Honeyfix thighbone lustmoan, she said,
        you're not dead.
you're just mixing your breath with mine.
Vodka on or off the rocks, and wine.

Fierce delight possessed us while sober
        and mischief of a puckish strain: we were alone
in the blues rain in the banjo snow
in the cold blow of the Smirnoff
and the Black Label.
We stood within each other on the porch
and encouraged the magnolias to explain.

She put her gluey lips to mine, absolutely,
        lipstick and vine,
someone grieving kissing a person
about to be dead in Tumble Down Town.
        Her not me.
A Catholic priest in her passion.

I know you're riding there,
        she said, country boy bred
to Tyneside Texas: all the moths flying
around the light in our head.

Hands palmed, each side
of the upturned face:
man nails on man's hands;
woman nails on woman hands.

Woke up this morning in bad Feral County.
Anne Sexton's detoxing palms all around my bluesy
broken
        and banged down head,
Alamo heart burned and betrayed,

mixing her breath with mine.

II

The smart of my heart over you
flows like levee water all over my scripts
and streams and wishes and dreams.

It begins to rain in the pepper groves
but will not drown in the storm drains
the strains of my George Jones dreams.

Learn, fix-it-head, cries the high lonesome
sound,
      learn Mr Maniac Blues
it swifts through the jacaranda trees, head
down to be educated O escape motif organiser,

it is time you bridled up and went, to go:

Horror damage consultant,
             heart bomb lover,
flick of the wrist terrorist,
             Mr Big Bang Fascinated,
drek tongue class act in the shadow of the mesa cast
by the lonely song you bring.

Fake casuals lack the urgency
I need to search all scorchings:
may their lethargy never cease.

Peace is a requiem without flowers
and now we're completely at war.
Funny things happen: you – me.

Feast upon this brotherhood
of spanner menders, smarm monkeys,
cross lingerers, stone rollers, fancy
Dans and O'Hara babes:

Here on the busted bottle porch and stairs
there is only one sunne to ride into
to smash our ever driven apology

for sleep to smithereens.

Your Love Is A Swarm And An Unbeguiled Swanne

So there you are lying down here breasts
                    abreast in the argent dawn
and I lust after you and love you.
The devil or the devil's disciple's
                    will not take my sucking lips.
He will not, will not, have thee: I will. I will put them with my lips
and your lips,
and they will meet and furnace the night and dawnlight
in Miltonic chill and heat
all fingers pointing.

There is something to real love indescribable.

Standing on a January morning hunched together on a gatepost
when snow starts
is like I hope heaven will be.
                    Faces just touching.
There is something about just touching
which is touching
beneath the start of morning birdsong, when peewits take off,
breaking from cover
and the musick of the becks and burns appear louder,
miles away from traffic,
and the sonata of the clopping of beasts through clarts.

There is a lightness
in this almost dark, snow brightening the fields, hardening the ground,
when fingers smoothly, keenly, without damage,
cause fantastic sensations within the people involved.

Damp moss on the palms of the hands.
Wet stile steps
and the slippery burn bridge. Careful now.

Winter hard thistle prick a real joy.

More snow and it's colder
but our hearts and minds are hotter
than ever before.

A dawn of many beings and things.

Strap Down In Snowville

O hello, Othello, black and green bastardo,
please be Mr Stepaside. I've arrived.
It is dark now and always dark.
And demons will step from that darkness.
I am the Pookah Swanne MacSweeney,
wingflap homme man, jalousie
my daily trade – my eternal war game
against you and the world, drunken to the last, flung
to the lost in the final Labour council-run
public toilet on earth.

All moons waned and keeled, peeled
of sanity and treasure of esteem,
lollbonce on black plastic rim,
bottle of Hennessy and a Football Pink,
's'all I need, unbuckled pants ankle-dropped,
now that the greenwood
is stacked for fire, and me the inebriate sodden slave, tree
destroyed by a legion of governments
and the studied stupidity
of the lapsed intelligence of the people of England.

It is dark now along the river and always dark
where we rievers and berserkers have our mad seizure way.
Who needs life, when you're sucking France's finest
and all the infogen necessary for amour of a breezy future
without ballooning liver count is strictly in the Pink?

Who here needs a bardic throne on Christmas Eve
in the tiled cubicle of magic marker messages – Proper
Gay Sucks: Ring this number. No Jokers Please?
's' all the reading I need before Harvey the Rabbit
arrives pushing his white fur balls in my swollen
face and the armies of rock-steady Goliath ants
in bent Durrutti Columns proceed righteous
from urinal drain under bolted door of this cuboid
cubicle paradise hell, up the wall and into my eyes.

It is dark now along my swan meadow river and always dark.
The shutters at Boots are coming down for Christmas
and my last chance to get better is going with the closing
of the electric tills.

We did not burn enough magistrates' houses. We executed
one king but did not drag out enough Tories, and hang them
from the greenwood tree.
These forever here in the snow-laden urinal are my hysterical
historical regrets. Swan Lud, get my poster, did you?

Freed from cognac bondage on anti-spasm Dr Dolittle
sweeties I'm Swan as I like under Elvet, wings awry
to bust a neck for once not quite my own in bent back
guzzle down fast mode.

                  I DIE HARD, Pookah Swoony
Sweeney Swan Ludlunatic, revelling Leveller without
sober reveilles to look for in the broken indices.
Your sleek torpedo cowgirl heels have gone again
and it is dark now along the weir and always dark.

You'll not return as long as I drink at fermented
dementing demesning streams. But I'm all set-up!
This is *my* toilet cubicle now! I can vomit as I like.

Clap hands, here come the tinselled demons now,
carolling away the broken night and broken angel me
myself I&I yours truly Bob's Your Auntie Mabel,
downed by cognacflak, Spitfire tailrudder flutter.
Bellyflop on Magwitch marshes, hollied demons
rise from methane mist in one Christmas cracker chorus:

Let's hear it for the fratchy fractured Geordie ploughboy
playboy, collapsed and weeping in his bent furrow.

Let's fix a bright planet from a parallel universe
unto his dead starre skyless recovery agenda.

Let's leave him in the auburn pools of piss in his
frozen kingdom cubicle with Santa's reindeers revved.

Let's poke out his kindly eyes of purest borage blue
so as not to shirk a Guernsey tomato face lying deep
in the frozen lake of the mirror.

Let's not brush but switch & broom his quivering
lids with tail feathers of garrotted larks, pollen of larkspur,

let's elect him chief celebrant and Mr Big Advisor
at the amazing red ant hoolie; aconite posies in his rotten head.

Let's book him into the spineyellow pages of forgetfulness,
under Giant Guzzle Unlimited Forever & White Knuckle Rides

To Nowhere Fast – Spectacular Passing Out Our Speciality.
Let's hit the digit snap arrival button so he cannot wipe the sick away.

Let's for auld lang syne and weird kindness' sake, hush our
bee-sting lips with fingers upright, tiptoe in the snow we go
and leave the slurry-loving, slurry sleeping lad alone.

Stripes on your shoulders, stripes on your back & on your hands.
Strips & stripes & little books & daddy's tearing flaring point of view.
Like it son, or cry bruised and fearing for the rest of your solemn.

Solo days away from the palace of portion plenty & peace. Exeunt smiles.
Snow on my forehead, snow in the lock. Snowfall tick-tock slowly
winding downwind arms adrift inside it like a clock.

Demons tongue-stalking, mouth-walking: they're talking
            East Berlin, talking Grunewald, looking
            at their Dalí watches on stiff drink wrists.
Crazy in capitals, dark star ferment: no thee at the go place.

Clap hands, here they come. Clapped bellhead, angel boyhood
to scarred bottledom, British West Hartlepool to Benidorm.
Snowblindness cover me, smother my waxy wiggle tongue.
Snow blow me. All the snow-wind's a berserk bugle
here in my closet kingdom on the rim of mad Noel.

Sober up tomorrow, clean shirt, shakefinger tieknot,
well-ironed, iron the drink out of my face, unbolt my self:
avoiding the Lost Chance Saloon in favour of Maybe
One More Choice To Make in the Department Store of Sighs.
Pick up a bargain, stride home with purpose through
the jigsaw snow and the ghost of all demon daddies
to sit feet up and watch It's A Wonderful Life on the telly.
Oh, yes. Certainly. No fulminations or bare excuses.
Yours soberly your favourite son miserable ever after.

Sweeno, Sweeno

Sweeno is two people – at least. Sweeno the night crawling homme man,
soaked sapien, gutter treasurer & curled up counter of cobblestones

in twitch vision. Nightjar Sweeno – bliss buster supremo Sweeno.
Sweeno the long cry rising like missile fins from the fans' end.

Eyeless child blind on the grim uphill road to courthouse
compensation claims and the blindness of eternal non-recovery.

Sweeno lathed and lathered with port-soaked Baudelaire gingercake
alone as nitrates usher from the gargoyle's twisted seizure face.

It is hundreds of feet in the air but it is a black mirror of Sweeno's
collapsed kitten lover's pansypetal printwheel pout. Swooney

Sweeno's beano, born on a booze cruise, Sweeno at the entrance marked
Out. Go go Sweeno the demons said as they dunked his fairy brain

and fried his head. Earn your bread like Barrymore before
you're dead, trashed the tuneful trolls in unparalleled register

& roguish misdemeanour. That's showbiz, Sweeno, you drunk Dan Leno.
Between foot and wing, Sweeno learned one vital thing: You cannot

be wolf or stag alone in taiga treeline forever, peltcrested
& snowhorned, harpstrung highly-strung up Swoonatic,

haunt of hard-nosed hornets underneath your bonny steelbonnet.
Learn early skinstrip and sell it by the rotten mile. Learn unsmile.

Sweeno the Olympian champ diver down 20 stairs half an inch
from a broken neck. Seaweed Sweeno the man on the rocks a wreck.

Yet there's another side to Sweeno, the man with eyes of borage blue,
the man high up in the heather hills with his Grace Darling, plover's

wingbeat driving his brain and snipe drums beating his heart.
The upright Sweeno whose streaming becks are a life's fuel. This

is not King Fool, prisoner in toilets armed with caustic cognac,
this is the prince of the northern air, with his tough tender love.

Feldspar finder, tickler of wild brown trout, bridger of burns,
man alive in love his heart in the skyblue sky, o heather o, Sweeno!

But really the truth is less poetic and palatable. This is the acid
bath boy, the angel with hissing meat right off the bone. Strong

tongued with viper juice, bamboo snake in jungle of his own
green many-fingered making. Mocker and mucker-up of true

love which dwells in a strong house. In perverse poise and perfect pose
he draws upon cynical strength of four Betty winds to see it down

into the grinding tumblestone quartz which splinters and thrills
in atomic smash-up as the devil grins inside his skull tornado.

This is the big riff: look out, look out, but don't beware for
you cannot step aside. Sweeno's black guitar's on fire in

the human cathedrals of sense. The strings used for garrotting
moths before fireflames can ever reach their secret wing dust.

Sweeno the freak born a year early 1947 and kept for questioning
in Area 51. Then Sweeno's far-out mind went underground into

every ravaged corner he could find that no-one else had touched.
Window-eyed and shutters down, fury festered in his fists

that execution plans for kings and queens and Tories had been
shelved. Greenwood tree over his stupid centuries skeletoned

into failed jigsaw of parched twigs and boughs. Failed opportunity
flailed his heart, Sweeno sick and resentful as brighteous righteous sin.

Yonder stalk the trance monsters dancing through the dark
distressing dew at dawn, demons holding babies, Sweeno's

Siobhan, leaving them upon the cold and open heartless
ground alive in itching gravel and grass with Betty blasts

of four winds to the heart. Sweeno's queeno in weep mode
when the ox-bow river of beauty busts its bushy banks

and all the riveted bridges Sweeno built can turn to mere rust.
Sweeno lying Lazarus in reverse on sick bed singing sickly:

Come down fleet rain and rinse my filthy dirty Betty soul.
Marry me to the chainlink fencing which like wild roses

extend their pricky pushy Jesus crowns into my vowbox bullet
tongue until strangled I&I like realo Sweeno me-o shall never rise again.

Sweeno sweating in the night, feeling the demon daddies his
flimflam framboise on ice cutting crew quiz his seizure bouncing

bedhead bonce raising the ratroof of his profane wordpush pillswallow
dickhead announcement zone, rawling on brain's hardbone basilica:

I AM THE NIGHTMARE. The blue tattoo legend bound to your Betty
sick soul forever. Kill that wasp. Beat it to death. O daddy demons, pin

its marigold and charcoal waistcoat stripes onto my Sweeno earholes,
lace together all its stricken wings for spectacles so I may read

again the many words of shattered vows, now I hear them struggle
into a storm of syntax once more as deadly distances which get

longer rise as steam from swamps here in the death-enclosing
night. No more for me the rising of a pink punk sun, black's

the colourway for Sweeno the Uncleano this very very day.
All separations yes, haul them in in blood-scrubbed bucketloads.

Fragments and distressed alphabets or arithmetic of misery
bound in distrust thrusts of gruesome guise laughingly we call

honour friendship and the universe. No rules now no greenwood
tree. The guillotines sent to Paris and none so near Sweeno's

hover handle hands. Not enough Ludlunatic posters pinned.
O please, Messrs Demon and Sons, vintage vintners and plyers

of slurtalk trade, pour Sweeno just one more before the heart
fails to grow and goes. Hear meano Sweeno: See what they did

to Elvis. Delilah haircut meets loss of power. Demon drink-up
death dribbles, absolutely, do take notes. No Samson Victor Manure

pillar push-downs. No push-ups but freely as the vomit streams
yanked by demon digits belly to basin. One day choke on it, tongue

jammed backward down throat's clogged highway. No noose good
news for those old escaping Tories. Enclosed meadows and one

executed king. Dreams so fierce, desert storms of ABC, all
fall down. One head enough. Not enough work done. Sweeno's

thin historical hysterical schedule in a spin. Sweeno in a mean
lean-to for Hurricane Betty: I've seen one hundred hungry dogs

crawl across their loved ones. I saw the skin fall from me
in steady strips and felt the sandpaper of so-called love

in eye of the very bone storm. I heard the wind say: I'm
blowing a mad and magic mojo horn and in the whipsong

of its Betty burned-out beauty – you call it filthy hatred and
betrayal for sad and solo Sweeno you are truly and completely

insane-o – I heard faintly from across the mountains far:
I'm going to lay down a thousand spells upon this unholy

disavowed ground until each writhing wily smiley wizard
downs his divining rods and realises finally at last at least

that they face a mixed trip back to Demon Town, and that
Demon Town is dead and Sweeno too will walk the line.

I'm afraid it is not possible, Sweeno in white strapjacket,
pilled to the nines, the nine winds, flung down the stairs

half inch from a noose-drop neckbreak in wake of Bettygate.
These are the lies, the footpad fingering falsehoods which

cannot nor will not, will not, will not, fall away rapidly
expiring. Falsehoods dark as my meadows are darkly dark

as the river and the roaring weir are dark & always dark.
When did you last see your father the insane interrogative

bells boomingly in his echoing bentneck at stairfoot as
another bottlebung pulled pop! right out and bolted down.

O chief stockholders in future equities of a rising thirst,
Sweeno is achieving major results in a shaky flaky market.

Sweeno cleans up and swallows down in dead of night
when others have gone home. He's a winning wino alright.

Don't doubt, deadly debt collectors all, look at the dividends
diving towards the rising expectations of a life in the sun

alliance, Sweeno's dalliance dance with death is legend now.
Sweeno's right there on the job. Pour him another and be grateful.

Anti-Lazarus Ludlunatic lolltongue Lollard, wine pourer
down his neck of night purrings, reports say Sweeno's

on the mend or round the bloody Beaujolais bend. Exit Rex.
No glory on the bottlefield overdrawn at the bottle bank.

Must have carpet experience. Presumably to roll king's
heads down the corridors of flexed power surge control.

The very trim, very slim experience of the twisted days;
days of yes I'm damned again and dimmed again by demons.

Days of bile man, slime man, vomit on his Texas shoes.
Glass glints purchase sunlight as birds and long-haul

planes fly through. Awful day, bad as any government.
Turkey plucker wanted – Norfolk. Head down the pan again.

What does it mean: to spew your ring? Sweeno, Sweeno,
you have vast experience of sickness – do you know, Sweeno?

No, no, no, hands up against any human requests at decency,
Sweeno's on his own-io, lone striker on his flat back four.

Ten years in the same team Going Nowhere Albion sponsored
not just match days Cellar 5, Victoria Wine, Threshers, Red

Wine Rovers, Plonk Park Disunited, The Old Dysfunctionals,
Soused Spartans, Inter Chianti's chanting demons' unflagging

fandom: Sweeno, Sweeno, give him a bottle he scores a goal.
Own goals mostly, catalogue of lost memory matches & scores.

Hands on knees and puffing hard I've had enough of this.
Ankle-tapping, broken bones, demonic shirt-pulling, the

92

beautiful game on the emerald field of dreams now turf
churned, filthy, white line I shimmy down impossible to see.

Chants, rants for Sweeno, zero hero. Come on ref, blow that whistle.
Rockets, fires and flags on trouble-free terraces. Ferocity

like mine. No-score draw. No extra time. No penalty shoot-out. No
golden-goal finale, no golden boot. Down the tunnel into nightlight. Endgame.

Up A Height And Raining

I

O just to vex me inside the bottle the wind stayed still,
and left correct my cheap Woolworth accoutrements.
Look at the sheep fleece from tumbler base, so finely
doused by rain from Garrigill, as I dance my demon tarantella
in the misty mire.

I stood on the hill with drenched face and soaking nerves,
ankle deep leaving the word sober at home, gobsmacked.
The upstream heather says more than I do, whispering
its purple blues.

I wanted it to blow tonight, to put it right,
to put my G-force twisted face back in place.

Brown leaves now on the beryl lawn

and the magpies are gone.

The golden rowan an ascending beam.
Arctic white roses from the Himalayas
white as the whites of my eyes used to be
before the demons held my lapels.

It is dawn and soon I will have a fit,
a seizure, a gagthroat convulsion,
a demon convention with furtongue
pressed hard against the roof of my mouth.

Mouth an estuary for the love of drink,
and I know I stink of it darling
and no amount of mints or garlic can hide it
from the houndsniff now that's built into your mind.

There will be blood, dearest, and horrid venom,
and black demon matter we'll never clean off.
I won't go again onto the drip. Not to the hospital
or the lock-away ward with its tightly kept key.
I'm going solo with capsules and the strength of your love.

Yes, love, they come: shiny shoes oddly enough,
the very nature of poetry erased from their report books,
tight black leather gloves to grip the bottles. Those
ugly gloved hands which search your soul.
You must guzzle aloud and let them do it
for every demon has to have its day.

My silence endless except for the swallowing.

O look at the golden leaves retrieved from the pink-sleeved trees
by the very act of the earth and its seasons.
They are bronze and gold, how very precious and horizontal
they are this regal collapsed November.
Look how they fall from the trees, quite drunk
with an unknown dream of renewal.

No stopping them and no stopping me
parallel to the horizon: my licence laws very strict –
I go from glass to glass, bottle to offy and back.
There's one thing you can say: I never slack
from TV cornflake zone until Big Ben's a post epilogue memory.

Except I can't remember it or anything
unless the mind-piranhas begin to swarm
and I know I am not Cromwell or Milton
but I am a Protestant heretic,
a Leveller lunatic, filled and felled by wine,
whose failed allotment is a museum of weeds,
whose rainy medallions are mare's tail and crowsfoot trefoil.

I do remember a blue light turning, and turning
to you and trying to speak and couldn't. Just
the bleeps on the machine trying to keep me alive.

And after X-ray escaping the wheelchair, vodka-legged,
felled face down by the drink in the street.
Nervous pedestrians leaning over
and a discerning passer-by: leave him he's pissed.

II

Perhaps I will rise in the fronds of Bengal
        crushed and tormented but determined to live
fantastically luxurious in the grandness of suffering
        searching for the lingering lips of her loveliness:
today I hunted through the wide wild skies,
not one finger to touch, not one sunshine dalliance alliance.

Arm rodded cloudward, always wanting the lightning mine.
I wanted to be the driver on the Leningrad train, screeching
        raptor of the whole northern air: sober groom with a bride.
Beasts steam and clop by the wire where my bottle is hidden,
        secret menu for peace, rage and change.

95

III

Yes, alcoholic, get him out of my face.

Gin in his nose he's a Christmas reindeer
every day he won't keep in his diary.
Holy mother, free him from my terrorised tree.
Release him from the twines of the briar,
see him flash to the cork in fen and fern.
Collapse him in misery. Slap him away.
Give him 45 per cent voltage and watch him go.

I am Sweeney Furioso, fulled with hate.
Hate for you, for me, hate for the world.
I eat beasts nightly and chew on snakes.

The blood of an invented heaven spills from my shoes.
I rage with wrecked harp
                                        for I am not the silence of Pearl
though she is inside me, like an argent moon.
I am a beast myself and return to see the mint die.
All that is left are drought-stricken stems.

There is no doctor cure.
There is no god and I believe it.
Every capsule in every brown bottle
is a pact of deceiving; the demons know.
Every prescription is a contract of lies.

I set my slurring lips against the stupid universe.
I squeeze my mouth as best I can around a bottleneck and mean it.
Daily I fix my redlight eyes against the raw law sunne
shaking my detox fists at the rams and lambs.
It will make me powerful if they flee from me.

Sorry is the last word in the long lost dictionary.
There was a man once, in a long thin box.
I see his washed out face in the fellside chapel.
We'll put out flowers and drink to his memory.
We'll scatter his ashes and drink some more.

The aim is victory over the sunne and to stand in a high place
holding a red flag
ready to lead unforgiven workers to righteous triumph.
You must execute kings and adulterous princes
and reserve the right to burn down Parliament.
Fight for your rights for the rest of your days.

IV

At Sparty Lea, here is the breeze burn,
at the bend in the bridge here is the stile squeak.
Here at the west window is the speaking for Pearl.

Here in the clouds is her eloquent silence
before addiction overwhelmed me and
made me silent myself. Her night cloud silence

following the clouds. And the clouds following
her and the light in her heart. She sails in
galleons of light all the way to Dunbar.

We seized the sky and made it ours, spelling
out the vapour trails: our clouds exclusively
before poetry was written, long before harm

and its broods of violence. Before we knew
the moon was cold and before men – real
men – stood upon it for the very first time.

But love, that moon, that moon is ours,
always, cold as your distant tongue.

V

Smoked salmon and lemon juice for breakfast,
      brilliantly chosen brewed teas!

The enticing slow lifting of garments, wearing
      and unwearing of black silk,

and exchanging of black and blue silks, white
lingerie chemise taken off as the mist rises
      to meet its handsome lover the sunne.

Underneath sheet lightning
               with audible thunder,
lightning down the rod and sceptre,
                  kisses fuming in darkness,
electric discharge between clouds,
                  fecund trenches & moss cracks.

Zig-zag bones and branching lines fully displayed,
                              diffused brightness to cooling toes
before unwinding unwounded stretches of sleep.
                              Kissed slumber barely awake
under the vast viaduct:
                              sex combs, complete claspness,
hairs locked and unlocked,
                              special pet favours given and received
on both sides.
                 Defying gravity.

Our passion, darling, is pure 1917. We ride
                                    the rods and rules and rails,
and skies for us will always be huge and authentic:
                              Northumberland Wyoming and Samarkand.

Fierce not the word to use for our kisses.
                              It is not fierce enough!
There are no wounds
                 and revenge and warfare will die in the mud
of an otherwise poor world.

Fireflies, conductors, heads limbs and hearts,
                 wires fixed to the great wide skies:

We diverted heaven's light
                              into sea or earth's true bounty

of our souls' brilliant kisses and everlasting starres.

Tom In The Market Square Outside Boots

Tom you're walking up & down the pill hill again.
Tom you're taking your moustache
to the Ayatollah doctor with his severe case
of personality drought.
Tom I saw you in the Heart Foundation shop
buying a cardigan five sizes too big.
Tom you're more bent over than when
we sat together in the locked ward.
Tom your coat is frayed like the edges of your mind.
Tom they let you out to the chippy but you're not free.
 Tom we're falling in the wheat
our feet betrayed by sticks and stones.
Tom we're in the laundry and it's us spinning
as they try to dry out our wet lettuce heads.
Tom there's a cloud on the broken horizon
 and it's a doctor with a puncture kit.
He's got a mind like a sewer and a heart like a chain.

Tom, who put the rat in the hat box?
Who gave the snakes up the wall such scaly definition?
Who plastered the universe with shreds of attempting?
Who unleashed the foes to annex your head?
Who greased the wheels of the Assyrians' chariots?

Tom the shadows of men are out on the river tonight
                                    reeling and creeling.
 Invaders from Mars have arrived at last
 and they're working in the lock-up wards.
 They're dodgy Tom, strictly non-kosher – just raise your hangdog
 blitzed out brain and look in the defenestrated alleyways
     which pass for their eyes.
 I suspected something in the fingerprint room
 & the sniggery way they dismissed our nightmares.
 Tom the door is opened
                          and you lurch down the path
     past the parterre and the bragging begonias
 but listen Tom
                 on the cat's whisker CB
                              listen Tom listen and look
 you're still a dog on a lead a fish on a hook

Tom you're a page in the book of life
 but you're not a book
  you're not the Collected Works of Tom – yet
there's no preface but the one they give you
  there is no afterword because no one knows you
  there's a photo on the cover but it doesn't bear looking at
    there's a hole where your family used to be
    an everlasting gap in the visitors' index
A SMILE FROM THE NURSES LIKE THE BLADE OF A KNIFE

    Tom – what happened to your wife?
    She used to visit – every Wednesday
    when buses were running before the cuts

    Now she's a lonely bell in a distant village
    sacked by the Government
    Mr and Mrs Statistics
                    and their gluey-faced children

    There's only one job on offer
    in the whole of Front Street
    delivering pizzas to the hard-up hungry

        and a spanking new sign on the unused chapel
        Carpenter Wants Joiners
    Jesus Tom it isn't a joke
        they crucified the miners
        with Pharisees and cavalry
        dressed up as friendly coppergrams
        it wasn't Dixon of Dock Green Tom
        it was the Duke of Cumberland and Lord Londonderry
rolled into one

        Dark today Tom and the city roofs argent with rain
        dark as a twisted heart Tom
        dark as a government without soul
        or responsible regard for its citizens

    trains' rolling thunder north and south over the great redbrick viaduct
    is the only sense of freedom I have today Tom
    the high lonesome sound of the wheels on the track
    like Hank Williams Tom we'll travel too far and never come back
    which is why they drug us to a stop Tom
    pillfingers over our fipples and flute holes
    we're in a human zoo Tom and it's a cruel place

Tom you're away from a haunt but furled in a toil
Tom there's a spoil heap in every village without a colliery
 there's a gorse bush on top you can hide in naked
but you can't escape the molten golden rays of the sky
bleaching the leukemia lonnens of ICI Bone Marrow City
Tom out here on the A19 the long September shadows of England
stretch from Wingate all the way to Station Town
long and strong and dark as the heart of the Jesus Christ Almighty
or the lash of the snakeskin whip he holds over us all

Tom are you mad by north-north-west
                    or do you know a hawk from a handsaw?
 Are your breezes southerly?
All the fresh air is quite invalid Tom and all the peeping spirits
have ascended to your brain
                              like region kites
and the gall of the world is mixed in a cup

Tom there's a silent flywheel on every horizon sequestered by law
                                        & severed from use

O dear, Tom, our heels are kicking at the heavens
sulphured eyebrows as we strike into the hazard universe of souls
where angels on our shoulders stand tall to make assay
for acid rain will fall and wash them white as snow
the weather has turned Turk Tom and we are almost ruined
 all softly cooling bright Atlantic winds from Cork and Donegal
are cancelled now
and fever has us in its grippy flame
ill-fit saddles have galled our wincing jades
            all that is left is the mousetrap of the devil
 but only if you give up on humans

 Tom invisible limers are fingering twigs in the groves
 Tom the twin sears of my hammered heart are set to be tickled
                    by leather-sleeved index fingers itchy and raw
 Tom there's a man in black with a lone silver star
 casting a shadow as long as his dreams

 Are your eyelids wagging Tom, so far from the burning zone?
 Have they fitted you out yet, did you have the bottle to object?
 Tom I can see you being folded like a linen tablecloth
 I can see the busy working hands working on you

101

We've been driven from the prairies Tom
              to an isthmus of disappointment
                          whose pinched becks can never sustain us

Tom I frighted my friends
              by getting this way
                          I sickled and scythed their garlands of wheat
tongue a runaway bogie with broken brakes
alone on the pavings written with rain I was a sacked village myself
palings downed and all fat fields returned to pitiful scrub
                          Station Town Quebec Shincliffe to No Place

              a network of underground ghosts
              bust at the seams

Tom will our dear decorated hangers be responsive to the hilts on the swords
                                                of our days?
          Will a tigerish revival leap upon us
                          from a leaf-locked lair?
          Will we be allowed another trample through mud?
          Tom I doubt it as the sunne doubts the starres.
          But starrelight is our single fire Tom, single
          and silver in the bed of the sky.

Brown-bottled venom and its work
                          a past prescription be
and all folded warriors
                          to gentle station grow.

The glow-worm dims and the sea's pearled crashy phosphorescence
in matin mist.

          There's a lark aloft in the morning Tom
                          its breasty song our autograph
          embracing fortune
                      in this out of focus world

                      high and mighty

                              and carried away on shields.

John Bunyan To Johnny Rotten

The long shadows of gold October stamped into the earth of England.
Amber crowns of trees shredded in the wake of the wind
whose invisible straps unwind allowing previously strapped grasses to become
unfleeced in air and have echoes and tunes like chapel hymns along the arm of
the law.
It is our rim of the world. It is our Aztec finality and birds fly there.
They are funny birds and bonny with aquamarine flashes down their pillowsoft
beakbone nearness & not like peewits at all.
It is our raining night & hoofing the wet lonnen. We are tearing down posters
at Loaning Head
pinned with one nail
and on the posters badly-drawn faces
for we are grey ghosts and silver surfers
the Finnbars the MacSweeneys the Pookas the Toms
the gun-carrying leadmineshaft knockabout nobodies
swimming beer off Sundays in the ice-cold tarn
never knocked down in Knock Down Town.
Nothing left in England now.
One king only not enough.
When did you last see your father is a laugh for me Tom, he was a jellied-eel traitor
to my poetic revolutionary heart
for always I have the axe in my hand. 1917. I have the hood and the axe and the
unsmilingness. I will do it as duty Tom, for waste must be punished.
O Tom, what am I saying?
I have wept before the shoals of shoes from Amsterdam, from Vienna, from
Warsaw, the leather straps and rusted buckles,
I wept before the Jewish mountain of shoes and sandals and encasements
purposefully stitched and modelled for feet whose feet-bringers were hoyed
in the ovens and the gas.
My axe alone Tom is against the oppressor & oppressors.
Tom, I'm not a poker-hearted Pooka. In sober raindawn reality I'm a cress-
hearted man.
No Caroline Louise no Hazel the pills are wearing off
I walk alive alone in Alston and lean against the menu of the Bluebell Inn
because it *is* mine. Smoke from the little trains are the fumes in my brain.
I walk there Tom, I run there Pearl. Rings to be made and vows to be said.
Tom, you have rockfire. Tom you have a lordly head.
Tom, can you hear the final slowing down spin of the flywheel
as the last cage ascends?
Tom, these are real men with faces like pandas
carrying badgerbrocks of coal. It's a memento now.
This place, Tom, *was* a nation, making trains and ships and cranes,

transporting unlikeables like us to the lands of boomerangs and redrock. Our
chainbroken fingers & hands acquainted with hunger & slavering slavery
kept together the hulks on the Thames, we were the true breath of the
nightforest noosehang land.
Tom, do you remember when lightly but enough to hear I knocked for you at
midnight, starres our only light, if starres there were? God help us Tom
we enjoyed it, one more Tory burned from his bed.
We stood together with tightly-bridled panting steeds among pooked sheaves
laughing until the sunne of togetherness warmed our roof-burning brand-
throwing shoulders.
How strong it was Tom, our amusement, as the red-coated militia arrived,
long before they drove down the miners in the villages. We blessed Jesus
the first Chartist for saving the bairns and the wife.
But the port-soaked Tory was dead, Tom,
and we sang our hymns with clean hearts.
Tom, nothing has changed except everything.

All of these centuries and centurions.
Tom, last night Milton & Cromwell said I should speak to you.
Bunyan smuggled a note on ragged paper.
Five knocks on the water pipe, I knew it was coming.
Tom, now it's us in the lock-up, in the spotty-face bathroom, in the lost
toothpaste universe,
in the argumentative wild Pearl honeysuckle wold unyielding unwielded world
of wrong-sized slippers, in the bad dressing-gowns
before harried relatives arrive to pull the armpits right, Tom, it's us: the walking
sandbaghead wounded dead of poor lost England.

I met Cromwell & Milton & Blake yesterday and they were lost as us,
funny stout men and one blind looking for the dreams of Albion.
Pen-ready men with quill of swanne.

Tom, you put your right shoe on your right foot and the left on the left.
The laces need to be tied and in absence of your apple-pie wife I'll do it
because bending down with firm fingers is so difficult
as pills plasticine your once-digitally correct hands and take the few straight
lines in your messed-up mind
and turn them into undriveable curves.

Even Blind Willie Milton even Cromwell even the Memphis Flash even
The Killer even Cash
is on a midnight Vincent Black Shadow.
From Huddie Ledbetter to de Kooning they're in slave overalls.
There's a pride in working for a living Tom, but it isn't for us. We're wasted
in wastelands before they were invented by Thomas Stearns Eliot.

Before Sylvia Plath paid her gas bill,
before Anne Sexton demanded blue disks from the doktor, before she
admitted an addiction to slavery & left us to be a spirit in the rainy trees.
Tom, King Arthur's in his counting house, counting out the wastage,
finalising the blame,
And who would say it, Thomas, who would lift the gall from the cracked glass,
but to say: Arthur, you too were a croupier of blame, you too
swept the table clean with the other social model, Margaret of St Francis?

Tom I do miss your wife Alice because for one reason at least
she brought us cloudy pastry tarts filled with apples from your trees
and sweetened by sugar from the Co-op in Langley Park
eating moon slices before pills travelled us to sleep
and Alice left sprightly rightly perhaps a purposeful heart searching for sunshine
in the darkness of day. Heart a mixed posse of love and not love,
of drawn guns and pouched bullets.

And a hatred of the Stasi experiment doktors shared by us all.

Tom, I want to lock the lunar lunatic's opal horns, I want to run before
the moon, I want to swing on my starres by Bunting, garlanded with squat,
I want to drink endless my Castrol to stop the stile squeak.
Tom, she's a princess of the mosswalks, and she does not want you to leave
her alone. And the bairns are crying for their dad, dad, lost dad, man with
moustache & a bone in his head.
Hard as a Birmingham spanner and right as a River Tyne rivet.
We're walking to the gay liberation centre, Tom, but we're already dead.

Taxi, Tom, heartsore, we're a pack Tom, infesting the age, thousands of thorns,
which may as well be pennies, someone to pay for it,
trainers for the bairns who know you're a photo once in the Sundays *borsik* in
the madman's paradise:
the club, Tom, the full-sized snooker table, where you can write in big chalk and
lay a fat man down: Tom, dear garlanded friend Tom, you're not that strong.

And if anyone picked on you, they'd have to peck at my fiststance darkdance first,
burst from the feldspar heifer hoof fields.
I am Lenz, underground my natural home. Watch me, Tom,
bust from the cowslip shadow alone with Pearl.

My heart and anger a double-barrelled sawn-off gun. Axe on hold whipped
clean by the wind from Pearl's mouth.
When did you last see your father, Tom can you help me?
Invisible he was forever when I was seven-years-old.
My canvas was clean but on it he put troubled colour.
Tom, the point is: I want that portion of him executed.

I know these hills so rest in my shadow.
I'll talk to the jailer and tea at dawn will be the leastest.
3764 Highway 51 South, Robert already having PASSED BY TO TOES
TURNED-UP TIME.
SURLY STEEL, BOLD STEEL, TUNNELS THROUGH ENGLAND,
TOM YOUR MIND'S LIKE MINE: PEASE PUDDING.
We're Navvies Tom. Straight up. Garlanded by bows of greenwood tree
and poem and lock-up ward and pill.

We are singing Milton today dreaming of Jerusalem
and the trains which never take us along the steel of the world.
Law with the wind in my face as I mince springingly princingly
on my wincing jade,
bit-jaw strapped in, fist-firm, fury in my heel spur and black frock coat
which can only bring death to the demons and the kings of frippery of England:

Law on the horizon and law in the lonnen at Loaning Head:
Stirrup-high I turn for the smell on the heather fellwind, still
on my mount, still but nostril light, honey of her thighs on Irish winds
before we gathered at night, building obelisks to Chartists
and we stroked goodnight the muzzles of upland high-hooved horses
because they reminded us of women lost in the dawn of the dew and dandelions

Tom I think I've gone turnip tuneless toes turned up frozen out from river
to rawness
on the rim of the law and the world
Tom a man came in a long black suit to saw off one of my limbs
before anaesthetic
Tom I pulled from my leather pouch – hole in its hiplength spout – a gun
with hammer of the finest steel, a curved knuckle-guard you'd wish to tell
your children about
if you lived beyond the rapes of the government

and Tom he didn't get any further
to you for example Tom because your brain's an oversteamed cauliflower
lolling in the Locomotive Arms
and my lover Tom my lover the poet is not a loader of rifles
a washer of signal cloths
she's a leader Tom she's a high-stepping jade herself
not one quick finger far from the pin

Tom, Pearl, I'm wedded to a theory from which I shall no doubt be soon divorced
in undainty circumstances
that disobedience
Disobedience, disavowal, the shredding of woofs and weaves,
the salivating of microphones
when all is denied, Bold steel low lot lacklevel.

I am these men and their lost women.
I am, spur-horsed, undenizened

Invisible twine plying merchants are unravelling the long grasses
and the plovering pull of the long windstrewngrasses pluck the prince
in his chest his heart his passion and love as if no tomorrow.

He caws, crows quietly, softly as a byre when beasts have departed
and rain on a shifted slate is like indescribable music which is
not music because the word is yet to be invented under the great heaven.
Let's wait for the very day Pearl says it whipped by rain. Beautiful Pearl.
And the leaves in the trees seem to whisper Louise because they're nuts Tom.

But I sank shaftshining in her budding cressbed. She's as wet as a 17-year-old.
They should be saying Michael Collins Bobby Sands and a litany a directory
in the wind from Sligo a stooked sheaf of telegrams of the dead the foolish
the aimless the aimed at the fallen and the framed Tom.
But they're not they're frozen like my angel in the fantastic magnet filings
of her boldly stirred heart.

So this is where you were in the he-boat the she-boat the he-she boast-come
together lover on the lake where the swans come in.
This is where the matin mount of your kisses wrestled with the oar-lock movings
for supremacy in the long mornings when the boat drifted into the reedbanks
This is where you rowed the he-boat and swam in the clear Irish water
and lay in his swanwings in the uncloaked unlocked dawn of padding
across the water
abandoned abandoned on the ferry landings of Ireland
pipes laid by for *Marie's Wedding* and *She Moved Through the Fair*
this is where my heart was a black kesh by the forlorn waves of the clear water
where the swans come
my heart my wooing MacSwooning whistling heart love
nothing but a black kesh in charcoal shadow on a sunless hill
I was a monster in Munster swinging my green jealous sword and making you pay

There were no telegrams Michael no messages Tom no letters the Royal Mail
is dead today but a bullet in the head and an army led by Judas
I do not believe him a good man

Soldiers need paying but he was not a soldier for freedom
only my heart will fight for her love and want nothing in return
but a kiss like a flutesong a hug like a tressed harp
a fire in her eyes and a dance in her hair
Tom there will be applause from the gatherings for the pressing and raising of heels
but it won't be for us
locked in the byre with the beasts and the winding gatepushing wind

Tom you know there'll be a wind from the west
all my life I've been a leader and now like you it's a lost soul department
nothing to say Tom but this poem
& the rare beautiful women of Doncaster beneath the High Street clock
Tom rarely sick
                              garlanded by sullen steel
Tom in the tunnel with the dynamite mob
and the jelly in his drainbrain
& mine
its gutters and flues of intelligence flowing away to a land filled with fairies

where Tom

rarely sick and rarely better
                                        threw doll from his pram
on gallery 10
where the screw was hanged with piano wire

we dawdled in the bronze-leaved sullen golden sleeves of the sike paths
threads of earth in the matin mist above the toy cathedral
edgewater clouded with invisible natural matter the human eye will never see
so you say for something to define it the water is clear to the bottom
pebble gatherings clear as the tumbler base seen through gin and vodka
brought by demons from the piggery where my heart lay in ruins
as now it lies ruined Tom
altogether Minister of Mayhem to Myself the great bombardier the single swanne

for she is swooning for his harpstrum lips all the way from the ferry landings
to the grid systems of New York and the sunsets of boulevards Tom
we shall never know with our bed end hangdog
broken busted barely visible beatitude
waiting the bolt to the temple
we're in a byre Tom it's true
                              and the transience of love hammers us all

and no swan call no flashing nuthatch

no rain on the gravel or mist in the hair
can save us from the eternal prospekt of the knacker's yard

red berries on the holly bushes Tom but we'll never see Christmas
there'll only be wreaths
not paid for by plastic
we'll never see Christmas

except with the angels

                    pulling us towards the argent arcs of starres
elegies unwritten left for those alive below

to argue and fuss over lost blood bones and brains

!GOD SAVE THE
QUEEN!